Home Downsizing
In Four Easy Steps

The Most Complete Guide to Home Downsizing Ever Published

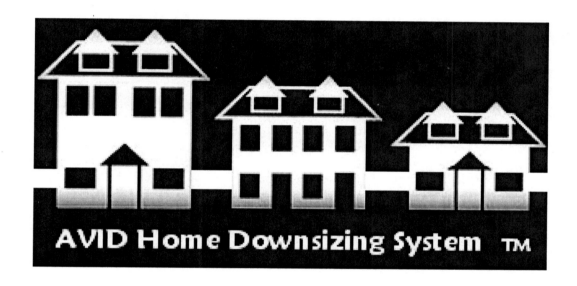

Michael Ivankovich, GPPA, MPPA
Home Downsizing Consultant

Home Downsizing
In Four Easy Steps

The Most Complete Guide to Home Downsizing Ever Published

First Edition, Copyright © 2009, Michael Ivankovich

Library of Congress Catalog Number: 2008910253
ISBN: 978-0-615-23261-4

Published by Michael Ivankovich, Doylestown, PA

Design and Layout by Susan Ivankovich, Doylestown, PA

Printed in the United States of America

Michael Ivankovich, GPPA, MPPA
Home Downsizing Consultant
P.O. Box 1536, Doylestown, PA 18901

Home Downsizing
In Four Easy Steps

Table of Contents

Introduction

Welcome to *Home Downsizing in 4 Easy Steps*. "*Home Downsizing*" is a term I am hearing with increasing frequency as I travel around in my job. I'm an Auctioneer. And I specialize in selling and appraising Personal Property.

What is Personal Property? It's a type of property that, by its most general definition, can include any asset other than *Real Estate*. The distinguishing factor between *Personal Property* and *Real (Estate) Property* is that *Personal Property* is movable. That is, the asset is not fixed permanently to one location as with real property, such as land or buildings. Examples of Personal Property include Antiques, Collectibles, Jewelry, Coins & Stamps, Furniture, Household Items, Pots & Pans, Knick-Knacks, Vehicles, Boats, Recreational Vehicles, etc. Personal Property is also sometimes called "*Movable Property*". Aside from your *Real Estate*, most of what you will be selling in the Home Downsizing process will be your *Personal Property*.

In my world, the four most common reasons people sell their Personal Property are referred to as the 4 "D"s:

- Death
- Divorce
- Debt
- Downsizing

This book will not necessarily focus on the first three "D's", although most of the content of this book would apply to those situations as well. Most days of the week I travel around visiting people who have an interest in consigning their *Personal Property* to Auction. With increasing frequency I have been hearing the term "*Downsizing*" when I ask them why they are interested in selling their *Personal Property*. And this term "*Downsizing*" doesn't seem to apply to any specific age group any more. Although I hear it most often from men and women aged 50-75+, I am hearing it increasingly from people under 50 as well.

Those of us in the 50 & above age group represent two generations of collectors, or accumulators, although we have saved for different reasons.

- For those adults of the *Great Depression* era (e.g., my mother), that group has accumulated and saved because they remember the days when times were difficult, and they learned to save things in the event things got bad again.
- For those adults in the *Woodstock Generation* (my generation, I'm 57 as I write this book), we collected things for a different reason. We grew to accept the sometimes mistaken belief that everything became more valuable as it got older. It didn't really matter what it was. If it was old, our goal was to buy it, keep it for a period of time, and sell it at some future date for a profit. We bought for investment.

So what we are seeing today is not necessarily one generation, but two generations of accumulators, who have large quantities of merchandise in their homes, who are getting ready to "*Downsize*", and who need to sell off their excess Personal Property.

But something quite unexpected has happened along the way that none of us ever anticipated. The generation that we expected would be buying our collections and excess Personal Property...*our children's generation*...simply doesn't want it today. They are not collectors or accumulators as we were. *"I've offered it to my kids and they just don't want it"* is an expression that I hear almost every day. Our children would much prefer the *cash equivalent* so they can buy the types of things they prefer, like *Ikea, Hi-Tech Cell Phones & Electronics, Pottery Barn, Mall Stores,* you know what I mean. And if it breaks, they'll replace it with something new.

This book has a number of specific objectives.

We'll Talk About the Home Downsizing Process and Setting Downsizing Goals & Objectives. The first major objective of this book is to educate you in the *Home Downsizing* process. Because before you can get ready to dispose of your excess *Personal Property*, you need to be perfectly clear on why you are moving, where you are moving, what you will be taking with you, and what you will no longer need.

- Are you moving to a new home, or staying in your current home?
- What are your *Downsizing Goals & Objectives*?
- How does the *Home Downsizing* process work?
- What are you keeping and what are you selling?
- We'll even provide you with *10 Sorting Categories* that will help you to clarify what you want to keep, and what you will let go of.

Valuation of Your Personal Property. What your things are worth in today's market, and how you can obtain that value, will be another major objective of this book. We'll help you to better understand the value of your *Personal Property* in today's rapidly changing market, and how to sell it for*:*
- The greatest amount of cash
- With the least amount of work
- In the shortest amount of time

How and Where Do You Sell Your Personal Property? What do you do with the excess Household Goods, Antiques, Collectibles, Collections, and Personal Property that you no longer want...your children don't want...and your children's *Generation* doesn't want? That will be another of the topics we will be covering in this book. We'll spend around 60 pages discussing how and where you can sell your excess *Personal Property*. You have more options than you probably realize and in this book we'll be discussing the advantages and disadvantages of the *10 Primary Selling Options* that are available to you. We'll talk about:
- The best ways to determine the potential value of what you are selling.
- Which selling options may be best suited for you.
- Assessing the time it may take to sell your Personal Property.
- The overall potential return you can expect after your *Personal Property* has been sold.

- Negotiating on price. You want to get as much as you possibly can, while the prospective buyer will be looking to pay as little as possible. If you learn how to negotiate properly you'll be able to put additional money in your pocket.
- And sometimes what you are selling is just not worth anything to anyone. The time and expense it will take to sell it simply isn't worth what it will bring in today's market. What can you do with those items? We'll introduce to you to the *Auctioneer* and the *Cleanout Specialist*. We'll talk about their roles, the services they provide, and how they charge for their services.

Preparing a Plan of Action and Executing that Plan: It probably took you 20-40+ years to accumulate all that you have to sell today. How do you set a *Plan of Action* that will enable you to dispose of it in a matter of only a few weeks or a few months? Once you have a better idea of what you want to do, and where you want to go, we will show you how to prepare a *Plan of Action* on how you may want to proceed. But preparing it will do you no good if you are not prepared to execute it. We will show you how to *Execute* your *Plan of Action* as well.

We'll Help You Get Through the Packing and the Move: After you've done your planning, after you've sold your excess Personal Property, it may be time to pack up your remaining belongings and move on to your next phase in life. We'll help you get there with *Tips, Strategies & Ideas* on how best to pack your *Personal Property*, how to select a Moving Company, and once you get it safely to your new home, how to unpack it all and get on with life.

Home Downsizing Tips: Along the way we'll provide you with more than *250 Home Downsizing Tips* that will help you to simplify the *Home Downsizing* process and maximize the return on the sale of your *Personal Property*.

But Most Importantly...We'll introduce to you to our *4-Step AVID Home Downsizing System*™. We have been dealing with *Personal Property* for more than 35 years. As an Auctioneer, Appraiser, Antique Dealer, Antique Shop Owner, Antique Show Promoter, eBay and Internet Seller, Author, Columnist, and even after a brief stint as a Cleanout Specialist, we know  *Personal Property*. We have seen that the vast majority of people have a hard time letting go of things, and they need a systematic approach when the time comes to downsize...and that is exactly what we have to offer. It is this *AVID Home Downsizing System*™, with each step building towards the next step, that will bring it all together for you and provide you with the tools and know-how you will need to move on to the next phase in your life.

And these are only some of the things we will be discussing in this *Home Downsizing in 4 Easy Steps* guide. There's a whole lot more in this book...so let's get started.

Chapter 1

Home Downsizing:
What Are You Trying To Accomplish?

If you are reading this book, you are probably considering a major downsizing or move in the near future. If so, you are not alone. A significant portion of America's 50-75+ age group is downsizing today. And why not? More than likely one or more of the following statements will apply to you:

- Your children are grown and gone.
- Your home has become an empty nest.
- You are retired, or getting ready to retire.
- You are ready to move nearer, or to live with, your children.
- You live in a home larger than you now need.
- The housework and yard are becoming too difficult to maintain.
- You are simply tired of the house and yard work and would prefer to spend your free time doing something else, such as traveling.
- Increased taxes and carrying costs are just becoming too much of a burden.
- You've lost a spouse or partner and are now living alone.
- You are ready to move to your shore house, mountain home, lake house, or otherwise smaller dream house.
- You would prefer to live in a year-round warmer climate.
- You are ready to tap into the home equity you have built up.

The reasons for downsizing are many. Each person's life tells a different story, but many of us have reached the same point in our lives. What we are seeing is the *"Grayification"* of America, and an entire generation who is getting older, who is ready to downsize, and who is ready to move on to their next phase in life.

Exactly what does the term *"Home Downsizing"* mean? Most likely it will mean different things to different people. Some definitions we have seen include:
- *Selling off excess Personal Property in order to make more room.*
- *Moving into a smaller, more manageable home.*
- *Cashing in on Personal Property investments.*
- *Reducing the mortgage payment and living expenses.*

Perhaps the simplest definition of *Home Downsizing* is *"Making Do with Less"*. It means shedding off all of the excess baggage that you have in your life including expenses, personal property, collections, or junk...and living a simpler, less complicated life.

Never lose sight of the fact that *"Downsizing"* is usually about the money. When a business *"Downsizes"*, it lays off staff in order to reduce

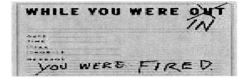

expenses. It divests itself of resources no longer needed and it cuts the fat, all in an attempt to increase operating efficiency.

"*Home Downsizing*" is no different. When you "*Downsize*" your home, you are basically seeking to reduce expenses, divest yourself of resources no longer needed, and cut the fat, all in order to increase your household's operating efficiency.

The ultimate objective of *Home Downsizing* for many is to increase the operating efficiency in your life, thereby giving you more money, with less work, and more time to do the things that you want to do.

Throughout the next several chapters we will be asking you a variety of *Home Downsizing* and *Personal Property* questions which are designed to help you to clarify what you are trying to accomplish in this downsizing process.

And throughout the book you will also be seeing hundreds of bulleted points which will contain *Information, Facts, Strategies, Tips,* and *Ideas* all designed to bring the detail of this book together and help you through the *Home Downsizing* process.

At this early stage the "*Home Downsizing*" process has two distinct meanings:
- *Downsizing, but staying in your current home.*
- *Downsizing, and moving to a new home.*

HD QUESTION #1: Do you plan on remaining in your current home, or do you intend on moving into a new home?

If you are "*Downsizing, but staying in your current home*", at least for a while, the *Home Downsizing* process will be somewhat easier. This means that at this point in time, your #1 objective is simply to make some room by disposing of the excess *Personal Property* that may no longer be needed or wanted, while preparing for an eventual move at some future date. The process outlined in this book will address your specific needs.

If you are "*Downsizing, and moving to a new home*", the process becomes more difficult. This means that not only must you dispose of your excess *Personal Property*, you must:
- Prepare to put your current house on the market.
- Look for a new home in the location of your choice.
- Make some harder decisions about what *Personal Property* you will be keeping, and what you cannot take with you, presumably to a smaller home.
- Select a Moving Company
- Prepare and pack for the move.
- Unpack and get settled into your new home.
- All within a time frame that may, or may not, entirely be of your choosing.

The process outlined in this book will address your specific needs as well.

HD Q*UESTION #2: If you are downsizing and moving to a new home, are you moving locally, or to an entirely new area?*

For most people, a local move will be easier than a long distance move. Although the move itself will be difficult, at least if you are staying local, certain things will probably not change, such as your *Friends, Doctor(s), Dentist, Accountant, Financial Planner, Church*, etc. Depending upon where you move locally, certain other things such as *Drug Store, Dry Cleaner, Supermarket, Restaurant(s)*, etc. may or may not change.

HD Q*UESTION #3: If you are downsizing and moving to a new home, what type of housing will you be looking for: smaller single family home, ranch or multi-level, townhouse or condo, apartment, 55+ active adult community, assisted living, modular or mobile home, etc?*

In the 1970's the average home was approximately 1,500 square feet with three bedrooms and one and a half baths. By 2007 the average home size was closer to 2,500 square feet, with many homes having extra-large kitchens complete with a preparation or cooking island, more bathrooms than occupants, spare bedrooms that now sit empty, a huge basement, 3-car garages, and who knows what else. With utilities continually rising and heating oil now approaching or surpassing $4.00/gallon, is it wise to continue maintaining such a large home?

For many, the answer is "*No*". According to *Money* magazine, 30% of their readers want less space, 23% wish to take the profit out of their home and move on, and 20% want to move where the taxes are lower. These reasons alone warrant *Home Downsizing*. Heating oil prices soared last winter, and natural gas is up nearly as much. Prices may rise even more this year. Combine this with the recent mortgage market change, with the value of homes going into a downward spiral in many parts of the country, *Home Downsizing* is starting to look a whole lot better to many.

But where would you prefer to move?

Smaller Single-Family Home: If you have been living in a single-family home, do you want to move into a smaller single-family home? For some the answer is yes. Some prefer the single family home, the more private and personal living space, the neighbors, and all that go with it. They prefer to have a smaller home (perhaps two bedrooms instead of four), with a smaller and more manageable yard, with lower taxes and carrying costs.

If you are looking at a single family home,

would you prefer a 2-story or multi-level home, or would a single floor ranch home be better suited to your current and future needs? And do you still want to be responsible for some yard work, even if it is a smaller yard?

For some, you will be able to purchase a smaller home with the profits from the sale of your larger home. Some will be able to live mortgage-free; others will have a significantly smaller mortgage. Either way, it's a step in the right direction.

If you do chose to buy a smaller single-family home, you'll probably be looking at a similar type of Homeowners Insurance as you have now. But a smaller home will probably require a lower premium, which should put some additional savings into your pocket.

For others, the days of the single-family home are over, and they are looking for a different type of living accommodation.

Condo or Townhouse Living: Moving from a house to a condominium or townhouse can be a big adjustment. When you buy such a unit, it typically means that you own your individual unit and a percentage of the common areas. Review (or better yet, have your attorney or financial advisor review) the condo/townhouse documents _before_ you purchase the unit. These documents include:
- Bylaws, Rules and Regulations
- Master Deed
- Master Insurance Certificate
- Owner's Association Financial Statements

Don't skim through these documents. Read them extremely carefully because they'll answer important questions like:
- Where does your ownership begin and end (i.e., sidewall, outside walls, porch, driveway)?
- What is covered under the Master Insurance Certificate? (Be sure that your Tenant Homeowners Policy picks up where the Master Insurance Certificate coverage ends.)
- How large is the Owner's Association's operating budget and financial reserves?
- How are trustees elected? Are they neighbors of yours or puppets of the builder?

Condominium/Townhouse Insurance is typically less expensive than the Homeowners Insurance on a single family home because you're no longer paying to insure an entire building. You're only paying to insure your contents.

Be wary of Association Dues. Typically most condo and townhouse associations charge a monthly association fee to cover the shared maintenance of such common areas as lawn mowing, landscaping, snow shoveling, the swimming pool, routine building maintenance, etc. Dues can vary from less than $100 per month to $500-$1,000+ per month. And it is not uncommon for some association dues to rise at more than $200 per month in a single shot, if the association has a specific, justifiable need for the additional funds. And larger flat dollar amount mandatory assessments (e.g., $5,000+ per unit) are not unheard of to cover major, unanticipated expenses (e.g., roof repairs).

At times understanding the fine points of the condo bylaws can make you big money. We know of a situation where a single unit in a 3-floor, 24-unit bayside condo was for sale. The true value was perhaps $125,000-$150,000 if in perfect condition. But the unit had issues. The condo was built on pilings, and this first floor corner unit was sagging slightly because several of the pilings had sunk. Repairs would have cost tens-of-thousands of dollars, and who knew what other problems lay beneath. The asking price was around $75,000, with no takers. The damage was obvious and no one was willing to take a chance, not knowing the final expense.

Then one day the condo sold...for around $60,000...to a developer. That developer had read the Condo Association Bylaws which clearly stated that any such structural damage was the responsibility of the Condo Association, not the individual condo unit owner. So he bought the unit at $60,000, forced the Condo Association to absorb the costly structural repairs, put a few thousand dollars into cosmetic improvements, and resold the property for close to $150,000, in less than one year.

Which proves that it pays to read your Condo Bylaws.

Moving to an Apartment? Renting Can Be Appealing: As a renter, you'll enjoy greater freedom than you did as a homeowner. If you sign a standard lease, you will only be responsible for paying the rent, while the landlord will be responsible for maintaining the building. If something breaks (e.g., plumbing, large appliances), you call your landlord, and the problem will (should be) resolved in a short period of time, costing you nothing. However, renting is strictly an expense, and offers no tax breaks as you probably had with your single-family home.

You will also save on your Homeowner's Insurance, since a *Tenant's Homeowners Policy* doesn't have to insure the physical structure, but only your *Personal Property*. As a result, your premiums should be lower.

Modular or Mobile Homes: Mobile Homes are prefabricated homes which are built in factories, rather than on site, and then moved to the lot or location where you will reside. The two most common sizes are *single-wides* (est. 18'w x 90'l), or *double-wides* (est. 20'w x 90'l). *Triple-wides* and larger are also available, but they are not nearly as common. They are transported by tractor trailers and deposited at your location. They can remain there indefinitely, or be moved to another location at some future date, if you so choose.

You can opt to purchase the land where your mobile home will be placed, or you can choose to rent the land in a trailer park or other location which may offer certain amenities not available elsewhere. That will be your choice, depending upon where you choose to live.

Modular Homes are also prefabricated in factories and transported to the location of your choosing. Unlike mobile homes, modulars do not have wheels and are not "*trailered*", but rather are transported on flatbed trucks.

One of the major advantages of mobile and modular homes is that they can be significantly less expensive per square foot when compared to on-site built homes.

<u>*Assisted Living*</u>: *Assisted Living Facilities* offer housing alternatives for older adults who may need help with some of life's daily requirements such as eating, dressing, toilet necessities, bathing, showers, etc. Certain facilities offer assisted living as the primary housing alternative. Others allow you to move into your own home or apartment today, but also offer assisted living alternatives if your health should change in the future.

HD QUESTION #4: What Do You Really Need House-Wise?

- Do you need a formal living and/or dining room, or are those rooms rarely used in your house?
- Do you need a state-of-the-art kitchen? Or have you been eating out more than in lately?
- Do you still need 4-5 bedrooms, or will 1-2 bedrooms do?
- Do you still need a home office?
- Do you still need a 2-3 car garage?
- What type of work area do you need? Garage? Basement? Outbuilding?
- Do you have any additional needs? Sunroom? Sauna? Jacuzzi? Small garden?
- Do you require any handicapped adaptations, such as a ramp, wider hallways or doorways, etc?

HD QUESTION #5: What about these additional factors?

- The proximity to family and friends.
- Access to medical facilities.
- Access to your Doctor(s), Dentist, Pastor, Priest or Rabbi.
- The yearly weather conditions.
- Access to parking.
- Access to airports.
- Access to social activities and entertainment.
- Can you take your pet(s) with you to your new location?
- Do you require stairs that are easier to navigate? Or a wheel chair ramp?

HD QUESTION #6: What are some of the primary *financial* advantages of *Home Downsizing*?

For many, the advantages of *Home Downsizing* far outweigh the disadvantages. For example, just a few of the financial advantages of *Home Downsizing* include:

- *Increased Cash Flow*: If you can reduce your monthly mortgage by moving into smaller quarters, you will most likely have additional cash left over at the end of the month to spend on the things that you want to spend it on.
- *No Mortgage*: By moving into a smaller, lower priced home perhaps you can tap into your existing home's equity, purchase your new home for cash, and live rent-free.
- *Lower Taxes*: Smaller quarters usually mean lower Real Estate and School Taxes, and they can all but disappear when you live in an apartment.
- *Lower Utility Bills*: With heating and utility bills rising, a smaller home is your best protection against higher utility costs, as you will no longer have to pay to heat un-used rooms. And if you move south, your heating bill will be even lower (although your air conditioning bill will probably increase).
- *Lower Homeowner's Insurance Bills*: A smaller home, of lower value, with less valuable contents inside, can cost considerably less than what you are paying for Homeowners Insurance in your current home today, thereby saving you even additional money.

HD Q*UESTION* #7: What are some of the primary non-financial advantages of Home Downsizing?

- *Less Housework*: Fewer rooms mean less cleaning.
- *Less Yard Work*: A smaller yard means less yard work. No yard may even better for some.
- *More Free Time*: A smaller home with fewer rooms and little or no yard maintenance can provide you with considerably more time to do the things that you want to do.
- *Less Stress*: A lower (or no) mortgage, less house and yard work, lower utility bills, and spending more time on doing the type of things that you want to do should reduce the amount of stress in your daily life.
- *Improved Quality of Life*: Downsizing can provide you with more time to do the things that *you* want to do.

HD Q*UESTION* #8: What are some of the disadvantages of downsizing?

- *Fewer Belongings*: Moving to smaller quarters will mean reducing the amount of personal belongings that you can keep, and disposing of certain things that may carry pleasant memories of years past.
- *Closer Neighbors and Less Privacy*: To some, especially those who have been living in a row house, townhouse, or apartment situation, this may not seem like a big deal. But for those who have been living with a great deal of privacy, closer neighbors may not be such a good thing.
- *Less Room for Guests*: Fewer bedrooms means that you will have less room for overnight guests, including family, friends, and even the grand-children. (A nearby hotel or motel can resolve this issue for you).
- *Space Restrictions*: Smaller homes mean less usable space. Living without a basement or garage might not be a good thing for a handyman.

- *Less Prestigious Living Quarters*: A smaller home in a less prestigious neighborhood may not matter to some. It will matter to others.
- *Change in Lifestyle*: If you have loved landscaping or gardening, your new home may not offer you the same level of satisfaction as the old home.

HD QUESTION #9: Who else should be involved In your *Home Downsizing* decisions?

One of the first major questions that you need to address at this point is who else should be involved in your *Home Downsizing* decisions? You are always ultimately responsible for making these decisions, but it is often wiser to bring in trusted family members, friends, or advisors whose opinions you respect and rely on.

We have found it best to involve these people early in the decision making process because it often avoids having to change direction to please a particular family member at a later date. It can also save you time and money long-term if you can avoid having to shift direction and re-do certain steps after you have already started the process.

HD QUESTION #10: What are your Goals and Objectives?

One of the first questions you have to ask yourself is *"What are you trying to accomplish by downsizing?"* Different people will be downsizing for different reasons. Why are *you* interested in downsizing?

- *Removing Memories*. Have you recently lost a loved one, through death or divorce, or does your current situation contain too many bad memories of better times past?
- *Removing the Excess Clutter*. Do you need to simplify your life by removing much of the accumulated clutter that is all around you, just to make more room?
- *Financing a Special Project*: Are you seeking to raise cash to finance a college education, reduce debt, buy a boat or recreational vehicle, or purchase a destination resort property?
- *Consolidating*. Are you consolidating two or more homes and need to remove the excess Personal Property? For some it means cleaning house after consolidating a family member's estate into their house. For others it means consolidating the Personal Property from a vacation home and permanent home into a single living situation.
- *Cashing In*. Are you cashing in the collections and Personal Property that you have accumulated over the past years, but no longer want or need?
- *Estate Situation*. Are you handling an estate that needs to be disposed of?
- *Moving*. Are you interested in moving into a different home or location?
- *Time Constraints*. Are you facing a time constraint because your current home may have sold faster than you had anticipated?

HD QUESTION #11: What are three things that you would like to accomplish during your Home Downsizing phase?

1. _____

2. _____

3. _____

Sometimes a downsizing move makes perfect sense. Other times, after further consideration, it makes less sense than you originally thought. There is an old carpenter's saying: "*Measure twice, cut once*".

There is also an old *Home Downsizing Consultant's* saying: "*Think twice before you move*". One of the major objectives of this book is to make you "*think twice*" before you make a move, and when you are indeed ready to move, to make certain that your move is a well-planned, organized, and downsized move.

HD QUESTION #12: Is *Home Downsizing* right for me?

Only you can answer that question. Better yet, involve people you trust into your *Home Downsizing* decisions. Your children, family, best friends, personal and/or financial advisors should all have some input into your decisions.

One of my favorite words is "*Synergy*". In its simplest form, *synergy* means that the overall product is greater than the sum of each of its original parts. Applied to your *Home Downsizing* situation, it means that you, with the helpful advice of trusted family members, friends, and personal advisors, will most likely make a series of better decisions than you could make by yourself, without their input.

> *HOME DOWNSIZING TIP*: Use the "*Synergy*" of advice from trusted family, friends, and advisors to help guide you through the *Home Downsizing* process.

HD QUESTION #13: When should you begin the *Home Downsizing* process?

Only you can answer this question but, in our opinion, the earlier, the better. We have seen all types of downsizing situations. Some people excel at planning and they have anticipated the day they will move...*years in advance*. They have slowly and methodically disencumbered themselves of all that they no longer needed, and were ready to move at a moments notice. These people are the exception, not the norm.

Most people don't want to face the realities that at some future date they will have to move. Although they know what has to be done, they put it off. But eventually, something forces the situation: sickness, loss of a loved one, the house sells far faster than expected, family needs, etc. Our recommendation is that you should begin the *Home Downsizing* process as early as possible, thereby relieving yourself from having to make potentially costly last minute decisions down the road.

HD QUESTION #14: What is the best way to begin the *Home Downsizing* process?

This will vary, depending upon each individual situation. The fact that you are reading this book is a step in the right direction. However, there are several very basic steps that most people seem to follow:

- *Housing*: Decide whether you will be staying in your current home, or moving, and what type of house you will need.
- *What to Keep*: Decide what you will be keeping, either for your new house now, or when you will be moving at a later date.
- *What to Give Away*: Decide what you plan on giving away to Family, Friends, or Major Donations.
- *What to Sell*: Decide what else must go, whether you are selling it, donating it, or dumping it.
- *What to Dump*: Let it go.
- *Move On*: Move on to the next phase in your life.

I know this sounds very simplistic, but these are some of the basic issues that you must address early in *Home Downsizing* process. Remember, your quality of life is not necessarily decreased by moving to a smaller home. We will be spending much of the rest of this book discussing these six steps in significantly more detail.

Now let's introduce you to the 4-Step *AVID Home Downsizing System*™ which will make the entire *Home Downsizing* process far easier than you ever imagined.

Home Downsizing Consultations: Many people feel comfortable planning and handling their own Home Downsizing chores. Others need help. If you would like us to lead you through the entire *Home Downsizing* process, or if you would like us to handle it all, from selling to packing to cleanout, contact us for further details:
www.HomeDownsizingConsultants.com

Chapter 2

Introducing the 4-Step AVID Home Downsizing System™

Home Downsizing can be a daunting process. Some of you have lived in the same home for 10 years, 20 years, 30 years, 40 years, and sometimes even more than 50 years. During that time you've accumulated a lifetime's worth of household items, Antiques & Collectibles, memories, and probably a lot of things that you haven't used or even seen for the past 30 years. But you still have them somewhere in your house, attic, basement, garage, or outbuildings.

We have more than 35 years experience in the Personal Property and Antiques & Collectibles fields, and during that time we have developed our unique *4-Step AVID Home Downsizing System™*...and we want to share it with you in this book.

And *AVID* is indeed a *"System"*. It is not a single stand-alone step, but rather four separate and complete steps that are designed to lead you from a houseful of excess *Personal Property* towards your goal of a downsized and uncluttered next phase in your life. In this chapter we are going to introduce you to the basic steps in the *AVID Home Downsizing System™*. And then in later chapters we will explain each of the four steps in considerably more detail.

In its simplest terms, the *AVID Home Downsizing System* represents four individual steps, with each previous step building to the next step. These four steps include:

1. **A**nalyze...Your Individual *Home Downsizing* situation
2. **V**alue...Your *Personal Property Assets*
3. **I**nvestigate...Your Selling and Disposition Options
4. **D**ispose...Of All Excess and Unwanted Items

And don't lose sight of the fact that the objective of these four steps is to help you to better understand how to simplify your life while selling your excess Personal Property in today's market for:
- The greatest amount of cash

- With the least amount of work
- In the shortest amount of time

STEP #1: *Analyze Your Individual Home Downsizing Situation*. You can't successfully downsize unless you understand how the *Home Downsizing* process works. In *AVID Step #1* we will:
- Discuss the *Home Downsizing Process*.
- Review your individual *Home Downsizing Goals and Objectives*.
- Analyze your *Personal Property Assets*.
- Introduce 10 *Categories* for sorting your *Personal Property*.
- Help you understand how you can benefit from the *AVID Home Downsizing System™*.

STEP #2: *Value Your Personal Property Assets*. Before you dispose of any *Personal Property*, you need to know what its worth. In *AVID Step #2* we'll discuss:
- The Mathematics of Selling *Personal Property*.
- Twenty different types of *"Value"*.
- How to determine what your items are worth in today's market.
- What's worth keeping…and what to let go of.
- What to do if you discover you have any hidden treasures.
- We'll get you moving in the right direction.

STEP #3: *Investigate Your Selling and Disposition Options*. You have more selling and disposition options than you may realize and you should use them to your advantage. In *AVID Step #3* we'll review:
- *Ten Selling & Disposition Options* which are available to you.
- The Advantages and Disadvantages of any of these options that may appeal to you.
- Few will use all ten options. Rather, you should view these as a *"Buffet"* of selling & disposition options, choosing only those that are particularly suited to your personal *Home Downsizing* situation.

STEP #4: *Dispose of All Excess Items*. This is where it all comes together. What's the best way to dispose of your unwanted and un-needed *Personal Property Assets*? In *AVID Step #4* we'll help you to wrap things up.
- We'll help you set a *Plan of Action* for disposing of your *Personal Property*.
- We'll help you create a *Disposition Schedule*.
- We'll show you how to *Execute* your *Plan of Action*.
- We'll make some final recommendations.
- We can show you what to do. Or, if you live in our general area, we can arrange to have it done for you.

Now let's continue with *Step #1* in the *AVID Home Downsizing System: Analyzing Your Individual Home Downsizing Situation*.

AVID Home Downsizing System Step #1
*A*nalyze Your Individual Situation

You can't successfully downsize unless you understand how the *Home Downsizing* process works. In Chapters 3 and 4 we will:

✓ *Discuss the Home Downsizing Process*: In this section we will continue introducing you to the *Home Downsizing* process and will begin focusing upon your individual situation and needs. Are you downsizing but staying in your current home? Or are you downsizing and moving to a new home? The answers to this and several other questions will lead us to the next section.

✓ *Review Your Individual Home Downsizing Objectives:* Each person's *Home Downsizing* needs are different. What are *you* trying to accomplish? Do you even know what you are trying to accomplish? In this section we'll try to get you thinking about your Individual *Home Downsizing* objectives, and how you can get it all done.

✓ *Analyze Your Personal Property Assets:* In this section we're not ready to talk numbers or place values on anything. Rather we'll begin taking a closer look at your *Personal Property* assets, and begin assigning them to one of *10 Sorting Categories*, depending upon whether you wish to keep it, give it away, or sell it. And for those items that you prefer to sell, we'll begin looking at where you might be able to dispose of these items for:
   o The greatest amount of cash
   o With the least amount of work
   o In the shortest amount of time

✓ *10 Sorting Options*: We'll introduce you to *10 Sorting Options* which are designed to help you get started sorting your *Personal Property*, and begin assigning it to categories that you may want to keep, give away, sell, or dump. We'll further define these categories as we progress through the process, and how you can adapt them to your needs.

✓ *Help You Understand How You Can Benefit from the AVID Home Downsizing System*: The *AVID Home Downsizing System* works. After you finish reading chapters 3 and 4, you will have a better idea how you can make our *AVID Home Downsizing System*™ work for you.

Chapter 3

Analyzing Your Personal Property Assets

In Chapter 1 we started this book by asking a series of 14 questions that were designed to introduce you to the *Home Downsizing* process and to help you better understand what you were trying to accomplish.

Once you decide that you are ready to downsize your home, and once you have a general understanding of the *Home Downsizing* process, the next step is to address the scope of your Personal Property assets, and decide what you want to do with them. At this point we are not really concerned about specific values. We'll address that in *AVID Step 2: Value Your Personal Property Assets*. Rather, what we are trying to decide here is *"What are you dealing with"*, *"How can you best handle it?"*, and *"Is it even worth handling"*?

Then in Chapter 4, we'll introduce you to a series of *Home Downsizing Strategies & Tips* that are designed to get you moving forward in the *Home Downsizing* process.

* * * * *

Rarity and Desirability: The first step in selling any *Personal Property* is to determine its level of desirability to other potential buyers. Will many other people want to own it, or is it valuable only to you? Was it hot in the 1980s but have prices softened today? (*"Softened"* is a nicer way of saying *"weaker"* than in previous times). Was it something that your generation could relate to, but your children's or grandchildren's generation has absolutely no interest in today?

As an example of a highly desirable category today, let's look at the gold and silver markets. It could be gold and silver coins, gold and silver jewelry, or gold and silver decorative accessories. As the price of gold and silver has moved upward over the past several years so too has interest in anything gold and silver. These items are extremely hot today, with many people interested in purchasing them, and willing to pay top dollar for them. If you will be selling items that are in such a highly desirable category, consider yourself fortunate.

Other categories have softened considerably, and are not as desirable as they were 5-10 years ago. Categories like *Country Collectibles, Depression Glass, Cut Glass, Ironstone, Longaberger Baskets, Shirley Temple* and *Dionne Quintuplets* collectibles, and many other such collectible categories are just not bringing what they did in previous years. These collectible categories still have many people interested in them, but prices have softened because as older collectors have moved on, they haven't necessarily been replaced by an equal number of younger collectors who value these items in the same manner as their parent's generation did.

And then certain categories are simply dead. *Beanie Babies,* most *1980's-1990's Baseball & Sports Cards, Collector Plates, Avon Collectibles,* and *Franklin Mint* or almost any other mass-produced *"Collectibles"* made in the 1980's-1990's are examples of categories that are simply dead. Too many of these items were produced for them to remain collectible today.

Condition: The next step in determining the level of desirability of what you are selling is to assess its *"Condition"*. The value of Real Estate is often defined as *"Location, Location, Location"*.

The desirability of Personal Property can be identified as *"Condition, Condition, Rarity"*. The reason we say this is that you can have one of the rarest and most desirable pieces of *Personal Property* but, if the condition is poor, non-working, or damaged…no one will want it. Rarity is important, but condition can even be more important. Good quality items are always in demand, regardless of the subject matter. Items that are damaged or blemished have little or no interest in today's market. Hence, *"Condition, Condition & Rarity"*.

How do you determine the <u>*Condition*</u> of what you have? Take a close look at it.
- Is the item working or non-working?
- Is it missing any parts?
- Is it a complete or partial set?
- Is it chipped, torn, stained, or blemished in any way?

In summary, *"Condition"* is absolutely vital in determining the value of your Personal Property. The better the condition, the higher of level of interest there will be in your Personal Property.

<u>*HOME DOWNSIZING TIP*</u>: *Rarity* is important, but *Condition* can be even more important, when determining value in many categories today.

<u>*Quantity*</u>: Another thing to look at is the *"Quantity"* of what you are selling. The larger the quantity, potentially the more valuable it will be, especially if the levels of *rarity, desirability,* and *condition* are all good.

A large collection would generally consist of a 50-100+ specific pieces, but the concept of *"large"* will vary depending upon the specific category. 50 beer cans, 50 match books, or 50 marbles would not be considered a large collection; 50 pieces of Kittinger furniture, 50 quality bronze statues, or 50 automobiles would be considered a large collection.

An important concept you need to understand about large collections is *"flooding the market"*. Sometimes it makes sense to sell a large collection in its entirety. Other times it makes sense to only sell part of a collection now, and then sell the balance at a later date. The theory here is that if too many pieces of a specific commodity hit the market at once, the average unit price can drop. But if the collection is split into multiple sales, the average unit price will be higher, thereby yielding a higher total price for the entire collection.

HOME DOWNSIZING TIP: Consider the impact of flooding the market prior to selling a larger-than-normal collection of anything.

Six Important Questions To Ask Yourself Regarding Your Personal Property

When evaluating your *Personal Property* assets, six primary Personal Property questions need to be addressed. We'll take them one-at-a-time.

PP QUESTION #1: What type of volume is involved?

Volume means different things to different people. I have seen people that weren't even phased by a houseful of merchandise, while others were overwhelmed by only several boxes. So in this step we need to get a better feel of the *"Volume"*, or amount of Personal Property that you are dealing with. What are we talking about?

- Closet
- Single Room or Multiple Rooms
- Attic
- Basement
- Garage
- Barn
- Out-building
- Entire House
- Secondary House
- Some or all of the above.

Volume doesn't necessary equate to *"Value"*, but rather to the *"Amount of Work Involved"*. A houseful of highly valuable items can be a good thing, a houseful of used furniture, sewing machines, hand tools, and chipped china might be a bad thing.

PP QUESTION #2: What types of merchandise are involved?

Next, take a closer look are the types of *Personal Property* you are dealing with. Usually there is something of everything in most households.

- Fine Antiques

- Quality Collectibles
- Larger Collections
- Quality Contemporary Furnishings
- Household Items
- Junk

If there is a considerable amount of *Personal Property* from the first four categories, from a value perspective this can be a good thing. If you are dealing primarily with Household Items and Junk, that is probably not a good thing.

PP *Q*UESTION #3: *What is the market level of what you are dealing with?*

- *High End*…the best of the best.
- *Middle Market*…somewhere in between.
- *Low End*…damaged, blemished or very common merchandise…the undesirable or the junk.

If you are dealing with *High End* items, that is probably a good thing. *High End* merchandise is always easier to sell because wealthy people always have money and are always seeking to acquire fine things. *Low End* merchandise, on the other hand, is never easy to sell. No one wants anyone else's junk…except the junk man. And the junk man is going to charge you to take it away.

Middle Market merchandise is not as clear-cut. Some of it can be very easy to sell; others no one wants it. It is difficult to be more precise in this limited space except that to say the *Market Level* of the merchandise that you are dealing with will be a major factor in its value and the ease with which you will have in selling it.

PP *Q*UESTION #4: *Are there any specialty collectible areas of value?*

This question focuses more upon Antiques & Collectibles categories because these are the primary areas that people collect. (We'll cover Household Items in PP Question #6). These categories are listed alphabetically, not necessarily in the order of importance or value. If you have items that fit any of the categories in this section, that could be a good thing and could be indicative of certain higher value areas.

- *Art & Prints*
  - Original Art
  - Vintage Prints
  - Limited Edition Prints
  - Unframed Art
- *Books*
  - Vintage
  - Collectible
- *China & Glass*
  - Better Names (too numerous to list here)
  - Mass Market (too numerous to list here)

- *Coins*
  - U.S. Gold & Silver Coins
  - U.S. non-Gold & Silver Coins
  - U.S. Currency
  - Foreign Coins & Currency
- *Dolls*
  - Antique
  - Modern & Collectible
  - Contemporary Mass-Produced
- *Firearms*
  - Antique & Contemporary Hand Guns
  - Antique & Contemporary Rifles
  - Accessories
- *Furniture*
  - 18th century Antique
  - 19th century Antique
  - Used 20th century
  - Named Contemporary 20th century
- *Jewelry*
  - Gold
  - Sterling
  - Diamonds
  - Other Gems
  - Estate
  - Costume
- *Militaria*
  - WW II, WW I, Civil War, etc.
  - U.S.
  - Foreign
- *Sports Cards & Collectibles*
  - Baseball - Pre 1970's
  - Baseball – 1980's-1990's
  - Other Sports
- *Stamps*
  - Philatelic
  - Postage
  - Collections & Accumulations
- *Sterling Silver*
  - Sterling (92.5)
  - Mexican (90.0)
  - Coin Silver
  - Other
- *Vintage Clothing*
  - Vintage
  - Early 20th century
  - Contemporary Designer Brands
  - Retro
- *Other*

PP Q*UESTION #5: Do you have any automobiles, recreational vehicles, etc?*

These items are often overlooked when sitting in a garage, barn or field, but they can have some very strong value remaining if the condition is good. Not too long ago we sold a 1939 Ford Woody Wagon for $47,300, which only months earlier had been sitting un-noticed in a farm field.

- Automobile(s)
- Boat(s)
- Camper(s)
- Jet Ski(s)
- Mobile Home(s)
- Motorcycle(s)
- Riding Mower(s)
- Tractor(s)
- Trailer(s)
- 3 or 4 Wheelers
- Other

PP Q*UESTION #6: What type of household items are you interested in selling?*

This is the area that frequently holds the largest potential of disappointment for many people. Used appliances and electronics generally will bring only a small fraction of what you paid for them, even if you purchased them only a short time ago. We'll discuss the reasons for this shortly. However, at this point you should recognize that although items in this area will have some value, for many individuals the value may not be worth the expense and effort that must go into selling them.

- *Appliances*
    - Washer
    - Dryer
    - Refrigerator
    - Freezer
    - Microwave
    - Other
- *Entertainment*
    - Television(s) – Flat Screen
    - Television(s) – B&W
    - Television(s) – Color
    - Televisions – Consoles
    - Victrolas
    - Stereo System
    - 33 RPM, 45 RPM, 78 RPM, other records
    - Cassettes, 8-Track Tapes, Beta, etc.
- *Furniture*
    - Used
    - Upholstered Sofa, Loveseat, or Chairs
    - Un-named Contemporary
    - Projects

- *Holiday Items*
  - Christmas
  - Other Holiday
- *Household Items*
- *Kitchenware*
  - Pots, Pans
  - Flatware & Cutlery
  - Dishes, China, Cups, Mugs, & Glasses
  - Baking & Cooking Accessories
- *Knick-Knacks*
  - Sometimes called *"Chochkees"*
- *Limited Edition Collectibles*
  - Prints
  - Franklin Mint
  - Collector Plates
- *Shop Tools*
  - Electric Tools
  - Hand Tools
  - Floor Tools
  - Painting Supplies
  - Accessories
- *Yard Tools*
  - Push Mower(s)
  - Trimmer
  - Yard Tools

After you have answered Personal Property Questions 1-6, you should have a better understanding of what you will be dealing with when it comes time to dispose of your excess *Personal Property*.

Ten Personal Property Sorting Categories

At this point we haven't yet started discussing values on things. But after you develop an understanding of what you have, the next step is to begin thinking about what you want to do with it. In the *AVID Home Downsizing System* we use ten primary sorting categories which are as follows. You are welcome to use some or all of them, of create any new categories that fit your personal situation.

- *Initial Dump*: What has absolutely no value, no one wants it, and can be dumped now, early in the *Home Downsizing* process, in order to create some additional space for you?

- *Keep It*: What do you want to keep for your next house and next phase in life?

- *To Family and Friends*: What do you want to give to family members and friends?

- *Major Charitable Donations*: What major items (Art, Antiques, etc.) do you want to donate to your favorite museums, institutions, or charities?

- *Sell It Privately*: What might be best sold privately, for a known amount of money, and without commission or moving expense?

- *Sell It On eBay*: What has potential national and international appeal and may be worth the expense and work of listing on eBay, whether by you or by an eBay Drop Shop?

- *Consign It To Public Auction*: What is worthy of sending to Public Auction so it can be sold in a competitive bidding situation?

- *Sell It At the Retail Level*: What has value and might be sold at a Garage Sale, Tag Sale, Flea Market, Antique Shop, or Antique Show?

- *Minor Donations*: Some things at this point may have no value to you, but might have value to such organizations as Red Cross, Salvation Army, Women's and Children's Groups, etc.

- *Cleanout Specialist or Dumpster*: What do you have left that might be of interest to the Cleanout Specialist? Or, now that all steps have been completed, should you simply dump it?

Remember that each of these categories are only temporary categories, and you have the option of moving any item to another category up until the day you finally dispose of it.

Home Downsizing Tips

✓ Before you proceed too far in the *Home Downsizing* process, you must first understand what you are trying to accomplish, and then define your personal downsizing goals and objectives.

✓ When analyzing your *Personal Property* assets, you must develop an understanding of the level or *Rarity & Desirability, Condition,* and *Quantity* of what you are selling, before you consider its value.

✓ *Condition* can be more important than *Rarity & Desirability* when determining what something might be worth.

✓ More often than not, *Quantity* equates to *"Amount of Work"* rather than *"Value"*. A large volume of average merchandise will generally equate to more work than value.

✓ Beware off flooding the market. Too many pieces of a specific commodity can sometimes cause unit prices to drop significantly if released into the market at the same time.

Home Downsizing Consultations: Many people feel comfortable planning and handling their own Home Downsizing chores. Others need help. If you would like us to lead you through the entire *Home Downsizing* process, or if you would like us to handle it all, from selling to packing to cleanout, contact us for further details:
www.HomeDownsizingConsultants.com

Chapter 4

Where Do You Start?
Home Downsizing Strategies & Tips

Up until the downsizing process starts, most people have been *"accumulating"*, i.e., buying things first for themselves, and then later in life for the children, and rarely throwing things away. Today the children are usually no longer at home, and you are probably no longer accumulating things at the rate you did earlier in life. In fact, for many this is the first time in their lives that they have really had to de-assess, or sell things off, in order to make more room.

It can be hard enough if there are two of you to share in the downsizing process. It can be significantly harder if only one of you will be involved in the process. For many the key is simply to get started. Once you get started, the process will go along more smoothly, and will even pick up momentum as you see yourself making some progress.

Remember, your ultimate goal here is to simplify your life. This chapter includes *50+ Home Downsizing Tips* designed to help you to get started in the *Home Downsizing* process, and to simplify your life. Subsections in this chapter include:
- *Planning Tips*
- *Getting Started*
- *Where Are You Going: Planning the Actual Move*
- *What to Keep and What to Dump*
- *Dealing with Family Members*
- *Downsizing Pitfalls*

Planning Tips
- *Home Downsizing Is Not An Easy Process*. Rather, it is an ongoing process, something that will probably take months to complete.
- *Take Your Time*. The *Home Downsizing* process does not happen overnight. It has taken you much of a lifetime to accumulate your houseful of assets and memories. Don't expect that you will complete the *Home Downsizing* process quickly.
- *Usually Plan At Least 6 Months Ahead*. As we said, this process will take time, both physically and mentally.
- *Planning Is Crucial*. Don't just jump into it blindly. Think about what you want to do, and think about how you can best accomplish what you want to do. Set a *Plan of Action*.
- *Develop A Sorting System*: Develop your own sorting system. Although we have recommended 10 *Sorting Categories* in Chapter 3, you should sort in any meaningful manner that works for you. Color-coded labels, magic markers, computer spreadsheets, keeping detailed listings, making piles, taking digital images can all be helpful. Use whatever works best for you.

- *If In Doubt, Keep It for Now*. Once it's gone, it's gone and you cannot get it back. You can always sell it at a later date if you change you mind. If in doubt, put it in the *"Keep It"* pile for now.
- *You Are Allowed To Change Your Mind*, Expect that you will change your mind many times over the coming months. One day you will want to keep something because of the memories attached to it. The next day you will want to dump it. That's perfectly normal and acceptable. You can change your mind as many times as you like. But place it in the *"Keep It"* pile until you are sure.
- *Double Your Initial Time Estimate*. Unless you are experienced at this, take your initial time estimate…and double it.
- *Remember That You Are In Charge*. Family and friends can, and should, have input with your decisions. However, you are the one who must ultimately live with these decisions. And you should be the final decision-maker.
- *Be Patient*. It probably took you 10-20-30+ years to accumulate all of the items in your home. Don't expect to dispose of it all in only a matter of a few days. It often takes many months to finalize a complete downsizing.
- *Don't Be Afraid To Ask For Help*: This process is easier for some people than others. If you are having a difficult time, don't be afraid to ask friends and loved ones for help.

Getting Started

- *Know Values Before You Begin Dumping*. *"Do Not"*, I repeat, *"Do Not"*, begin dumping anything before having someone look at it for potential value. All too often things that you perceive as having value turn out to be valueless, while things that you perceive to have little value end up having considerable worth. Before tossing anything out you would be wise to hire someone who is knowledgeable in *Personal Property* to provide you with valuations prior to beginning the dumping process. A *Professional In-Home Personal Property Walk-Through Valuation* is usually a good place to start for most individuals. A *USPAP Appraisal* will be more precise and detailed, but will cost significantly more because of the time involved in its preparation. The up-front cost of either should seem quite reasonable when compared to the potential loss if you throw the wrong things away.

- *Start Early In The Process*: Whatever you do, don't wait until the last minute to get started. Start early, work in smaller blocks of time, and the job will go much easier.
- *Start With A Small Room*. Start by selecting a small room to begin with. Once that smaller room has been successfully completed, it will be easier to move on to a more complex room.
- *Start With A Room That Has Less Sentimental Attachment*. A bathroom, closet, or kitchen may be a good place to start. The most important thing is to start somewhere, and then build momentum towards larger projects.
- *Start With Larger Objects*. It's often easier to start by eliminating larger items, such as furniture. The logic here is that you can begin to feel as if you are making progress after only making a few decisions.
- *Start With A Portion Of The House That You Don't Currently Use Much*. A grown child's empty bedroom is often a good place to start.
- *Start With Personal Papers and Family Photographs*: This won't gain you that much space, but it can be fun, and is a logical step in starting the downsizing process.
- *Work In Limited Blocks Of Time*: The process can be very tiring and emotionally draining. Limit yourself to only a few hours at a time, at least in the beginning. Then, if you are feeling up to it, you can work in extended periods of time.
- *Stick With A Specific Project Until Done*: Once started, do your best to complete a specific project, especially smaller projects. For example, if your start cleaning out a closet, finish that project before moving on to another project. However, recognize that larger projects, such as a basement or attic, will most likely not be completed in a single session.
- *Anticipate The Weather*: Plan ahead, keeping the weather in mind. You don't want to work in the attic on a scorching July day, and you don't want to be working in the garage or outbuildings in sub-freezing weather. Use the weather to your advantage.
- *Give Yourself Ample Lighting*: Little will get done if you can't see what you are doing. If the room you are working in isn't bright enough, bring in some temporary lighting to brighten up the workspace.
- *Give Yourself Ample Workspace*: You can't sort much into piles or sorting categories on a single, rickety folding card table. Try to provide yourself with one or more solid 3' x 8' folding tables. Today's tables have light, plastic tops and are much easier to move by yourself than the heavy wooden tables of previous years.
- *Use Heavy Duty Plastic Bags For Dumping*: It doesn't matter whether you buy them at the supermarket, home improvement store, or dollar store, be sure that you use heavy duty plastic bags for packing old clothes and linens, or dumping unwanted smalls into the weekly trash. Nothing is more frustrating than having a lighter-duty plastic bag break after you have spent considerable time packing it.
- *Homes With More Space Can Sell Better*. Selling off your Personal Property can make you even more money when you sell your current home. Clutter tends to make a house look small. By downsizing before you put your house on the market, you can make your house look even bigger than it really is, thereby increasing its salability. We know of one situation where the Real Estate agent felt that a house brought $30,000-$40,000 more than it would have brought had the home downsizing not occurred.

31

Where Are You Going? Plan Your Move to Your New Home.

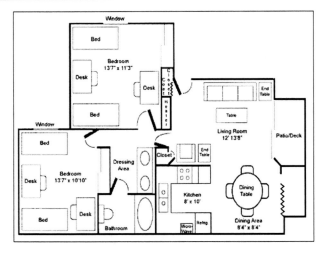

- *Visit Your New Home...Several Times... Before Moving In.* You will often miss things on your first visit, and see things on later visits that you missed in your first visit.
- *Take Pictures Of Your New Home Prior To Moving In.* This will help you to remember the sizes, spaces, nooks & crannies that you will be trying to fill.
- *Get A Floor Plan Of Where You Are Going.* This blue print, complete with each room's size, will help you to better visualize what you can...and what you cannot...take with you.
- *Plan Where Special Pieces Will Go.* Recognize what simply will, and will not, fit.
- *Visualize Your New Living Environment.* Tag those things that you will definitely be taking with you, which makes it easier to see what you cannot take with you.
- *If Appropriate, Hire Someone To Help You.* It's sometimes easier to work with outside parties rather than family members. Outside parties can be less attached and can help you to move forward.
- *Recognize That Storing Un-Needed Things Can Be Expensive.* We know of one family that spent more than $30,000 in storage locker fees over a period of several years storing a deceased brother's furniture and Personal Property assets because they had a hard time letting go. When they did finally send the items to Auction, they netted less than $5,000. Throwing $25,000 away was probably the last thing that their deceased brother would have wanted. Don't be afraid to let go.
- *Recognize That Moving Things Twice Can Be Expensive*: Why should you pay someone to move something that you no longer want or need? First, you're paying the moving expense of putting it on the truck, and if your move is based upon weight, you are also paying for the weight. (We'll talk more on this in Chapter 21). If you no longer want or need something, dispose of it before, not after, the move.
- *Look For Furniture With Double Uses To Save Space*: Sometimes simple planning can save you space in smaller quarters. For example, a futon or sofa bed can provide you with extra sleeping space for that occasional overnight guest. A trunk can double as storage space and a coffee table. And a slant-front bookcase can also serve as your bill-paying desk.
- *Double Moves.* You should be aware that some moving companies can perform a *"double move"* for you. For example, if you are sending some things to Auction, they can load those items onto the moving van first, and those items that are going to your new home on the back of the truck. They can then move you into your home first, and take to remaining items to Auction...on the same day. And by using the same truck, you can save big money in moving fees.

> _HOME DOWNSIZING TIP_: _"Double Moves"_ can save you big money in your move, and you should ask your mover how they can accommodate you in this area. However, you need to be well-organized in order to take advantage of the _"Double Move"_ cost savings.

What To Keep and What to Dump

- _Keep the Items You Treasure The Most_: Certain things will mean more to you than others. Keep the most important things in your life, and never let them go.
- _Think In Terms Of Four Levels Of Disposition_.
    - o _Tell The Children To Come And Get Their Items_. All too often your children, whether intentionally or unintentionally, use your home as free storage for their un-needed items. Call them first, and give them a deadline to remove their items.
    - o _Get Rid Of The Junk_: If for no other reason than to make some room, and to feel as if you are making some progress.
    - o _Sort The Better Items Into Two Categories:_
        - ▪ Those you are taking to your new home
        - ▪ Those you will be disposing of prior to your move.
    - o _Keep Sentimental Objects in the Family_. Pictures, knick-knacks, travel mementos, etc. will rarely have much value in the secondary markets. Give them to family members, friends, or better yet grandchildren, who will someday enjoy and appreciate them. It will make you feel better in the long run.
- _Sell The Balance After You Move In_: After you have had a chance to settle into your new home, you can dispose of any excess items that you now know you will no longer need.
- _Be Realistic About What You Are Keeping_: A good rule of thumb is that if you haven't used it in several years, or if you forgot that you even had it, it's probably time to let it go.
- _Consider Donating Major Items Now_: If you are considering donating any major items, e.g., a major piece of art to a museum, now is the time to start the donation process. It takes time to learn whether the museum is interested in acquiring your donation, and then it takes even additional time to complete the appraisals, legal

work, and IRS paperwork necessary to capitalize on the tax advantages of the donation. (See Chapter 16).

- *Before Dumping, Consider Alternative Charitable Causes*: For example, you can donate clothing to a Woman's Abuse Center or Homeless Shelter; books can go to your local Library's Fund Raising Sale, used furniture can go to Fire Loss Victims. Also consider the Red Cross, Salvation Army, your Church, other Churches, as well as local Agencies and private Non-Profit Groups. The list can go on. Regardless of the tax advantages, before dumping anything think of how your excess items can help those in need.

- *Shredding Personal Documents*: If you don't already have one, consider purchasing a shredder. As you are cleaning out you will undoubtedly come across certain personal documents (tax returns, pay stubs, personal financial information, and perhaps even some old love letters). Shredders are quite inexpensive and can keep some of your sensitive personal information from falling into the wrong hands.

- *Important Additional Questions To Ask Yourself Before Dumping:*
  o When was the last time you used it?
  o Do you really need it?
  o Can something else you are keeping substitute for this item?
  o Can you get by without it?
  o Will it fit in your new house?
  o Can you use it in your new house?
  o Do you know someone else who could use it more than you?
  o Does it need to be repaired?
  o Is it in good shape, or is it about ready to break?
  o Do you really care about it?

Dealing with Family Members

- *Discuss the Downsizing Plan With Children & Family*. Involve your trusted family, friends and/or advisors in the process early. Remember the concept of "*Synergy*" as it applies here.

- *Have Your Will Current and Up-To-Date*: Consider letting family members know what's in your will...ahead of time...in order to avoid future problems.

- *Let the Family Know How They Can Help*. If the family wants to help. let them. Invite them in. More often than not it will make your job easier.

- *Have Family Members On-Board Before Starting*. One of the worst things you can do it start the process without family input, and then have to change direction in order to please family members.

- *Share Important Details With Trusted Family*: Let trusted family or friends know where you may have important things stored or secured, e.g., bank accounts, jewelry, your will, or other special assets. Should something unexpected happen to you, ultimately these items will revert to the government if your family is unable to lay proper claim to them.

- *Agree on a Family Distribution System that is Fair to All*: Most children, and even grandchildren, have at least one sentimental item in your house, e.g., a piece of jewelry, artwork, furniture, book, etc. Try to devise a plan where everyone gets at least one item to remember you by, or at least something from your current home.

- *First Come, First Served*: One system that we have seen work is that each person gets to put their name on one item, and the first name on that item gets it. This system also works to get people to your home quickly, before the best items are taken.

- *Names In A Hat*: Another system that we have seen work is that family names are put in a hat. First name drawn gets first choice of the available items, and so on.
- *Encourage Everyone To Be Fair*. You may have to play the peace-maker, or negotiate some types of settlement at times. But the system should be intended to be fair to all.

Beware of These Home Downsizing Pitfalls
- Failure to understand how difficult and sensitive a process this can be for some people.
- Failure to talk through your personal goals and objectives, and to make sure that your goals and the family's goals are compatible.
- Failure to agree on what "*fair*" means to all key players.
- Assuming that each of the decisions you will make will have the same meaning, or lack of meaning, for everyone.
- Failure to understand the various approaches to dividing things up.
- Failure to manage conflict. Recognize that some conflict is normal. Take your time. Don't rush things.

* * * * * * * * *

AVID Step #1 Summary

This is the end of *AVID Step #1*. Between Chapters 1-4 our objective was to introduce you to the *Home Downsizing* process. In these chapters we:

✓ Introduced you to the *Home Downsizing* process.

✓ Reviewed your individual *Home Downsizing* goals and objectives.

✓ Analyzed your *Personal Property* assets.

✓ Introduced you to 10 *Sorting Options*.

✓ Introduced you to the *AVID Home Downsizing System*™.

If you like what you've seen so far, let's move along to *AVID Step #2* where we'll address the *Value of your Personal Property Assets*.

In *AVID Step #3* we'll *Investigate the 10 Selling and Disposition Options* that are available to you.

And then in *AVID Step #4* we'll discuss how you can *Dispose of Your Excess Personal Property Assets* by *Creating* a *Plan of Action*, and then *Executing* that *Plan of Action*.

AVID Home Downsizing System Step #2

Valuing Your Personal Property Assets

Before you dispose of anything, you need to know what its worth. In Chapters 5-7 we'll discuss:

✓ *The Mathematics of Selling Personal Property*: Chapter 5 will be a short chapter, but in it we will introduce you to the selling formula you will use when selling your *Personal Property*.

✓ *The Many Different Forms of "Value" in Today's Market*: You will probably be surprised at the many different types of "*value*" you may encounter when selling your *Personal Property*. In Chapter 6 we'll discuss twenty different value types, and which value types you should expect to receive when selling your *Personal Property*.

✓ *How Do You Determine the Value of Your Personal Property?* We'll tell you here and now that it is extremely difficult for most individuals to determine a realistic current market value on each item in an entire house by yourself. Most people will need a *Professional In-Home Personal Property Walk-Through Valuation* or the help of a certified appraiser or an individual who has considerable experience in valuing *Personal Property*. But for those interested in trying to do it yourself, in Chapter 7 we'll introduce you to 16 free and fee value resources that may enable you to do the job yourself, including:
   o Price Guides
   o Trade Papers
   o Reference Books
   o Free & Fee Internet Value Sites, and Much More

✓ *What's Worth Keeping...and What To Let Go*: You need to recognize that certain things will have considerable value to you because of the memories attached to them. But without the memories, they will have little value to anyone else. Other factors such as technological obsolescence and changing generational tastes will significantly reduce the value on many items that you paid good money for only several years ago.

✓ *What To Do If You Have Any Hidden Treasures*? Most homes have certain items that will have significantly more value than you may realize. How do you get obtain top value on these items? We'll tell you.

✓ *We'll Get You Moving in the Right Direction*: Remember, the *AVID Home Downsizing* process is a "*System*". It is a series of four steps which build upon each other, and which are designed to take you from the beginning to the end of the *Home Downsizing* process. By the time you are done with this *AVID Step #2*, you will be well on your way to reaching the finish line.

36

Chapter 5

The Mathematics of Selling Personal Property

This will be a short chapter. But the concept included here will be the key to how much of a profit you will make when selling your *Personal Property*. The *Mathematics of Selling Personal Property* is not very complicated. And what you *paid* for something has absolutely no bearing on what you can sell it for today. I repeat: *Absolutely none.*

If you are selling Antiques or Collectibles, you will still most likely see a fair return on your investment...*if you bought wisely*. Some categories are hotter than ever, most are somewhat *softer,* and some categories are simply dead.

If you are selling household items, tourist mementos from past vacations, children's toys, personal belongings, or 1980's-1990's newly made *"Collectibles"* (e.g. Franklin Mint, Collector Plates, Baseball or Sports Cards, etc), you will most likely see a return of only pennies on the dollar.

But the bottom line is this:
- If you no longer want it.
- If your children don't even want it for free...

...it is most likely that few others will value it very highly either.

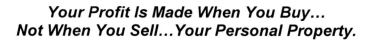

Your Profit Is Made When You Buy...
Not When You Sell...Your Personal Property.

How did you obtain your *Personal Property*?
- Did you inherit it?
- Did you receive it as a gift?
- Did you buy it shrewdly at Auction?
- Did you buy it Retail, but were a good negotiator?
- Did you buy it at full Retail price, without even asking for a price discount?
- Did you buy it when prices were low, or at their peak?

Although what you paid for something will have no bearing on what it will <u>sell for</u> today, what you paid for your *Personal Property* will be an extremely important factor in ultimately determining your *profit or loss* when selling your items.

If you inherited what you are selling, or received it as a gift, you will obviously make money because your cost basis is zero dollars. The question of *how much money* you will make will be determined by how skilled you become at selling through the right venue and/or negotiating the best price. But if you *purchased* your *Personal Property*, which most of us have, several other factors come into play.

The *Mathematics of Selling Personal Property* for a profit is quite simple:

The *SELLING PRICE* of the *Personal Property*
LESS the *COST OF GOODS SOLD* of the *Personal Property*
LESS the *SELLING EXPENSES* associated with selling the *Personal Property*
LESS the *TIME VALUE OF YOUR LABOR* in selling these items
EQUALS your *PROFIT* or *LOSS*

Let's try to clarify this formula.

- *Selling Price*: This is the amount you actually receive for the property you sell. You want to sell it for as much as possible; the buyer wants to pay as little as possible. Usually your selling price is somewhere in the middle. As an example, let's assume a Selling Price of $1,000.

- *Cost of Goods Sold*: This is what you paid for the merchandise. If you bought smart, and bought better quality merchandise, in a desirable category, you will most likely make money. If you paid high-retail, or if you purchased middle market merchandise (translation: very common items, or items having condition issues), you will make less of a profit. And if you collected a category that has little or no market interest today, you will probably lose money. As an example, let's assume your cost of goods sold is $750.

- *Selling Expenses*: This includes all selling expenses you incur when selling this property. Some examples of selling expenses are listed below. In our example, let's assume $100.
  - Advertising
  - Commissions
  - Cleaning or Repair Fees
  - Moving Fees
  - Postage & Shipping Fees
  - Referral Fees
  - Etc.

- *Time Value of Your Labor*: This is one concept that most people fail to consider when valuing their profit or loss, and it represents money you may have lost doing other things, while your time was diverted selling this *Personal Property*. For example, if you are retired, have time on your hands, enjoy doing what goes into selling things, this number would be zero dollars. However, if you must forego working at your full-time or part-time job in order to sell this *Personal Property*, you may be losing big money. For example, if you have a job that pays you $50 per hour, how many hours do you want to waste selling something that will only bring you a small amount of money. In these instances, you are probably better off selling it quickly, sending it to Auction, or hiring someone to sell it for you. As an example, let's assume that it took you 5 hours to sell this *Personal Property*.

- *Profit or Loss*: This represents the final amount that you actually made, or lost, when selling the personal property.

For example:

Selling Price:	$1,000
Less Cost of Goods Sold	- 750
Less Selling Expenses	- 100
Net Profit	$ 150

Now consider the value of your labor. In this example, assuming that you earn $50 per hour, and assuming that it took you 5 hours to sell this Personal Property, you would have theoretically lost $100.

Net Profit	$ 150
Less Cost of Labor (5 hours at $50/hr)	- 250
Net Loss	- $ 100

If you value your time, always remember to take the *"Time Value of Your Labor"* into account when selling your *Personal Property*.

* * * * * * * * *

Home Downsizing Tips

✓ What you paid for something will have no bearing on what you will be able to sell it for in today's market. Absolutely none.

✓ Your profit is made when you buy your Personal Property, not when you sell it.

✓ You should always factor the *"Time Value of Your Labor"* element into the Personal Property selling equation. Failure to do this could end up costing you money instead of making you money.

Chapter 6

Understanding Value: What's It Really Worth?

"What type of Value are you looking for when you sell your Personal Property"? I have seen many confused looks when I first ask this question. *"I just want to know what my things are worth"* is the most common response.

"Value" is perhaps the most misunderstood word in the entire *Home Downsizing* process. What is something truly worth? The word *"Value"* will mean different things to different people. Sellers want to sell their *Personal Property* for as much as possible, while buyers want to pay as little as possible. Both parties can look at the same item, and have different perceptions of value.

<u>*Fair Market Value*</u>: *Fair Market Value* is the term that most people think of when they consider what their items are worth. *Internal Revenue* Regulation 1.170A-1(c)(2), defines *Fair Market Value* for donation purposes as:

> *The price at which the property would change hands between a willing buyer and a willing seller, neither being under any compulsion to buy or sell and both having reasonable knowledge of the facts.*

Treasury Estate Tax Regulation 20.2031-1(b) furthers defines *Fair Market Value* as:

> *The price at which the property would change hands between a willing buyer and a willing seller, neither being under any compulsion to buy or to sell and both having reasonable knowledge of relevant facts. The fair market value of a particular item of property includable in the decedent's gross estate is not to be determined by a forced sale price. Nor is the fair market value of an*

Department of the Treasury
Internal Revenue Service

item of property to be determined by the sale price of the item in a market other than that in which such item is most commonly sold to the public, taking into account the location of the item wherever appropriate.

Therefore, *Fair Market Value* is a *hypothetical number* and not a fact, and it assumes that items are *not* sold, but rather that ownership in the item is retained. *Fair Market Value* is most commonly used to determine a decedent's gross estate tax on items that are not sold upon the decedent's death, but rather are bequeathed to the decedent's heirs. (Property that is actually sold will be taxed based upon the actual sale price). *Fair Market Value* is also the form of value used to substantiate tax deductions for non-cash charitable contributions (e.g., donating a piece of art to a museum).

Market Value: *Market Value* is similar to *Fair Market Value* in certain ways, but different in other ways. Whereas *Fair Market Value* is more of an IRS definition of value, *Market Value* represents more of an appraisal-related definition of value. One definition of *Market Value* would be as follows:

> *Market Value means the most probable price which a property should bring in a competitive and open market under all conditions requisite to a fair sale price, the buyer and seller each acting prudently and knowledgeably, and assuming the price is not affected by undue stimulus. Implicit in this definition is the consummation of a sale as of a specified date and passing of title from seller to buyer under conditions whereby:*
>
> 1) *Buyer & Seller are typically motivated*
> 2) *Both parties are well informed or well advised and acting in what they consider their own best interests*
> 3) *A reasonable time is allowed for exposure in the open market*
> 4) *Payment is made in U.S. dollars or the equivalent*
> 5) *The price represents the normal consideration for the property sold unaffected by special or creative financing or sales concessions granted by anyone associated with the sale.*

Note here that *Fair Market Value* assumes that title is not transferred, while *Market Value* assumes that title is transferred.

While *Fair Market Value* and *Market Value* are often good barometers for value, they can often be unrealistic value objectives on many items in the real world. These values can point you in the right direction, and can help you to understand whether your item is "*Common-Unusual-Rare*" or "*Good-Better-Best*". But remember that both are theoretical numbers, not facts.

- They consider a longer exposure time prior to sale, something that may not be applicable to your personal situation.
- They may force you to accept higher carrying costs, something that may not be applicable to your personal situation.
- They may force you to incur higher selling costs, something that may not be applicable to your personal situation.
- There is no guarantee that your item(s) will sell for *Fair Market Value* or *Market Value* within your allotted time frame.

Value, Cost & Price

Let's continue our discussion with three very commonly used terms that relate to value: *Value, Cost* and *Price*. Don't they basically mean the same thing? Absolutely not. Each term has its own meaning and its own definition in the discussion on value.

- *Value*: It's a difficult term to define because it is not a fact, but rather a theoretical term, or an *"Opinion of Worth"* if you will. Value is a measure of worth on the future benefits anticipated to accrue because of ownership of a piece of property.
- *Price*: Is the amount of money the seller is <u>asking</u> for a piece of property. Price is a fact. It is what someone is <u>asking</u> for something at a specific point in time. It has no real bearing on what an item will eventually sell for. And price can fluctuate and change at the seller's discretion.
- *Cost*: Cost is what a buyer has <u>actually paid</u> for a piece of property. This is not an opinion of value. It too is fact. Cost represents what someone has paid for something at a specific point in time.

So you can take the exact same piece of Personal Property, and its *"Value"*, *"Price"*, and *"Cost"* will most likely be three different numbers.

Market Types

Value can also be determined by the market in which an item is sold. In the world of *Personal Property*, there are four distinct markets, and the value for any given item will vary, depending upon which market the item is being sold in.

- *Retail Market*: A *Retail Market* is the market where items are sold at *"Retail"*, i.e., to the end consumer. Examples of retail markets would include Antique Shops, Art Galleries, Jewelry Stores, Department Stores, Consignment Shops, and other types of retail establishments. Sometimes eBay, Amazon, and other Internet venues operate as Retail Markets. Sale price is usually (but not always) highest in this market.
- *Wholesale Market*: A *Wholesale Market* is where wholesalers sell to the trade (i.e., those who purchase with the intent of re-selling). Antique Dealers typically pay *"Wholesale"* prices when buying privately from the public, hoping to re-sell the merchandise at *"Retail"* prices, thereby making a *"Fair Profit"* for their time, labor, and cost of investment. Sometimes eBay, Amazon, and other Internet venues operate as Wholesale Markets. Wholesale Market price is typically lower than in the retail market.
- *Orderly Liquidation Market*: An *Orderly Liquidation Market* is a market in which property is regularly sold in an orderly and advertised fashion, but for which nominal time constraints apply. For example, there is reasonable exposure time (but not a prolonged exposure time) before the goods are ultimately sold. Final sale price can vary considerably in this market, and can at times be higher than in the retail market. *Public Auctions* are a good example of *Orderly Liquidation Markets*.
- *Forced Liquidation Market*: A *Forced Liquidation Market* is a market where property is sold quickly, within a very restricted exposure time frame, and typically

without regard to whether it is the "*most appropriate*" market for what is being sold. Tax Foreclosure Sales, Bankruptcy Sales, or Storage Locker Auctions are all examples of *Forced Liquidation Markets*. Sale price is typically the lowest in this market.

Primary and Secondary Markets

Another concept you need to understand when considering the value of Personal Property is whether it is being sold in the "*Primary Market*" or "*Secondary Market*".

A *Primary Market* is a market in which new items are still being created by the manufacturer and are available for sale for the first time. Computers, appliances, and furniture are good examples of items being sold in a *Primary Market*. *Hummel* figurines purchased directly from *Goebel*, or *Byer's Choice* figures purchased directly from *Byer's Choice*, or original artwork purchased directly from the artist, or a gallery representing the artist, are also examples of *Primary Market* items.

Some characteristics of *Primary Market* merchandise are:
- Brand new and never-used condition.
- Original packaging, with original paperwork and instructions.
- Guarantee and/or warranty applies.
- You have the right to return it if not 100% satisfied.
- In perfect condition. And if not perfect, it can be returned to the retailer or manufacturer for a refund or exchange.
- Financing may even be available.

A *Secondary Market* is a market in which items that are still being created by the manufacturer are being resold to subsequent owners in another market. Examples would be contemporary appliances and electronic items being resold via classified ad on *CraigsList*, or *Hummel* or *Byer's Choice* figurines being resold at Public Auction.

Some characteristics of *Secondary Market* merchandise are:
- Used condition; sometimes perfect, and sometimes not.
- Probably no original packaging, paperwork, or instructions.
- Sold "*As-Is*" without guarantee or warranty.
- Cannot return if imperfect or not in running order.

Obviously buyers will value merchandise bought in a *Primary Market* higher than merchandise bought through a *Secondary Market*. And this is an extremely important point for those who are downsizing to understand: *Almost all of your merchandise will be sold in some form of Secondary Market, and your merchandise will generally only bring a small percentage of what a brand new version would bring today.*

HOME DOWNSIZING TIP: Much of your excess *Personal Property* will be sold in some form of *Secondary Market,* and more often than not it will sell for far less than what a brand new version would cost today. Be prepared for this.

Appraisal Values

One of the biggest mistakes people make regarding value is to take an *"Appraisal Value"* as gospel or fact, without understanding what an appraisal is, and who is providing that appraisal.

First, let's define an *"Appraisal"* or *"Appraised Value"*. As we said above, *"Value"* is a theoretical number. It is not fact, but rather an opinion of fact.

An *"Appraisal"* is nothing more than the *"Opinion of Value"* issued by an appraiser. Ask ten different appraisers to appraise a single item, you will probably receive ten different values, and often these will include a wide range of values. *"Why"* you ask, isn't there a single value for a single item. There can be many different answers to this question:

- Some appraisers are more knowledgeable and experienced than others.
- Some appraisers are experts in some areas, and with limited knowledge in other areas.
- Some appraisers prefer to use *"Conservative"* (lower) appraised values, while other appraisers prefer to use *"Feel Good"* (higher) values in their appraisals.
- Personal Property values change over time, both increasing and decreasing, like the value of a stock, depending upon a wide variety of market factors.
- Different appraised values are used for different purposes.

Verbal Appraisals: Most people love receiving *"Free Appraisals"* but you must never lose sight of the fact that *"You get what you pay for"*. When you receive a *"Free Appraisal"*, you will most likely receive a self-serving appraisal, or a *"Feel Good"* value (a value designed to make you feel good, but probably on the very high end of what you can reasonably expect to sell it for).

When you go to a jewelry store and ask the jeweler for the value of your diamond ring, unless you are paying that jeweler for a written appraisal, the jeweler will most likely tell you what the ring is worth to them, at that precise moment in time. If you walk out and then return, the *"Appraisal"* can change. It most likely represents a price that they are willing to pay, knowing that they will be able to make a fair profit without doing too much work. The number the jeweler gives you is not what they are going to sell it for, but rather what they want to buy it for. Does that represent a true *"Appraisal"*? Of course not.

Antiques Road Show Appraisals: Although the *Antiques Road Show* has been a tremendous commercial success for PBS, it has caused nightmares for Auctioneers and Antiques Dealers. Why? Because most of the items shown on the *Antiques Road Show* are pre-selected because they are expected to have a wide appeal to their viewers. And the minute the *Antiques Road Show* tells someone that their chest of drawers is worth $25,000, everyone watching that show assumes *"I have one that looks just like that, so mine must be worth close to $25,000"*. The fact that theirs is Empire and not Chippendale in style, that theirs is mid-19th century and not late 18th century, that theirs is pine and not Cuban mahogany, that theirs has condition issues, and no provenance, has no bearing on value, at least in their eyes. And when an Auctioneer or Antique Dealer tells them that their chest of drawers is worth no more than $300-$400 in the real world, the owner feels that they are being cheated. *My advice*: Watch the Antiques Road Show for the entertainment value, not the appraised values. It can only lead to disappointment.

Antiques Road Show-style Appraisal Seminars are usually not much better. Typically some non-profit group will bring in a *"Qualified Appraiser"* and charge perhaps $5-$25 per appraised item, with all proceeds going to benefit that group or organization. These appraisals are verbal, not written, and are not binding on the *"Qualified Appraiser"* or the organization, and frequently results in a *"Feel Good"* number.

I once had the unfortunate experience of having an individual bring in a small consignment for Auction, which included a book having a few color lithographic plates. Without my knowledge he had been told at an appraisal event that the book was worth $100. When the book sold for only $5 at Auction, the consignor was livid. He had been told that the value was $100 by a *"Qualified Appraiser"*, and by us letting it go at $5 (to the highest bidder, mind you), he felt we had cheated him. He wrote a nasty letter to the Auction Company and never did business with us again.

Actually an appraisal is more detective-work than anything else. The appraiser will basically take a good look at an object, analyze its key characteristics, investigate what other similar objects have sold for in the open market recently, make adjustments to value based upon such factors as differing size, condition, color, and style, make additional adjustments to value based upon such factors as rarity, provenance, documentation and relative importance when compared to other similar items…and then issue their *Appraised Opinion of Value.*

Appraisals by Friends & Acquaintances: More often than not the worst form of *"Appraisal"* you can receive is a well-intended *"Appraisal"* by a friend. These appraisals are typically based upon such reliable market research as *"My brother's neighbor's cousin had one that looked just like yours, and they were told ten years at a free appraisal event that their's was worth $xxxx. Yours must be worth twice that today"*. This is not the type of *"Appraisal"* that you can have much confidence in. I said it earlier, and I'll say it again: *You get what you pay for.*

USPAP Appraisals: Written Appraisals, completed in compliance with *USPAP* (*Uniform Standards, Professional Appraisal Practice*) guidelines, are typically the best appraisals you can receive. Although they will cost you an appraisal fee, *USPSP* appraisers much follow a strict code of appraisal guidelines that insure you will receive an appraised value that is fair, honest, and un-biased.

Insurance Appraisals

The real world definition of *Insurance Replacement Value* is *"trying to stick it to your Insurance Company"*. This is because *Insurance Replacement Cost* typically represents the highest form of value. *Insurance Replacement Cost* means that if your insured item(s) should become lost, damaged, destroyed, or stolen, the Insurance Company must pay you the amount necessary to replace your lost/damaged item with a comparable object. And under some policies the costs of locating such an object (travel time, consultant fees, etc.) may also be covered under your Insurance policy.

Aren't Insurance Companies concerned about this? To a certain extent yes, but to a certain extent no. For several reasons. Insurance Companies always try to pay less than your original claim. *Claims Examiners* are nothing more than clerks who must follow the Insurance Company Claims Rule Book which dictate how claims must be handled. Lower level clerks can handle claims up to a certain amount. Higher value claims are pushed up to more experienced *Senior Claims Examiners*. Even higher value claims must be handled by, or at least approved by *Claims Supervisors, Claims Asst. Managers, Claims Managers, Claims Directors*, and in larger value claims, the *Vice-President of Claims*.

The purpose of each level of the *Claims Examiner* is to minimize the claim amount paid by the Insurance Company. And they are very effective at this because Insurance Companies know from experience that most claimants don't really understand the claims process. The more confusing the claims process, the more *Claims Examiners* that the claimant (the person who filed the claim) has to deal with, the more likely they are to cave in and accept whatever the Insurance Company offers, in order to settle the claim and move on with life.

Here is a dirty little secret. Insurance Companies <u>like</u> to insure inflated values on Personal Property...*because they can charge a higher premium for that Insurance*. Insurance Companies have *"Actuaries"* whose primary job is to look at past claims experience ...*Premiums Received, Claims Paid*, and *Related Expenses*...and devise a premium that will insure that the Insurance Company will make a profit.
- If claims are as expected, the Insurance Company makes money.
- If claims are higher than expected, the Insurance Company still makes money, just not as much.
- And if claims are lower than expected, the insurance Company will make a lot of money.

The point here is not to attack Insurance Companies. Rather the point here is to make certain that you understand that any *"Insurance Replacement Value"* appraisal that you may have received will probably have no bearing on what you will be able to sell your item for in the real world.

Salvage Value and Scrap Value

Let's talk about a few additional forms of *"Value"* before wrapping up this chapter. *Salvage Value* is defined as:

> *The amount of money that could probably be obtained from the sale of an obsolete item or a damaged item for which repair is neither desired, possible, nor economically feasible. The repair cost would exceed the item's worth.*

Examples of items having *Salvage Value* could include damaged automobiles being sold to a junk yard for parts (hoods, tires, doors, etc.), or a dated computer that is sold to a computer repair shop for parts (RAM, motherboard, keyboard, etc.).

Scrap Value is slightly different from *Salvage Value* in that it represents:

> *The amount of money that would probably be received for the sale of a piece of Personal Property that is meant to be broken up for the remaining value.*

Good examples of items having *Scrap Value* could include damaged Sterling Silver candlesticks being sold to a scrap dealer for the value of the sterling, or damaged jewelry being sold to a jeweler for the price of the gold or gem stones.

Some Final Forms of Value

Book Value: The value listed in a particular Price Guide or Reference Book (this will be discussed in the next chapter).

eBay Value: The price that something has actually sold for recently on eBay.

Internet Value: The value of something that has sold recently on the Internet, or on a Web Site other than eBay.

In Summary: Obtaining *Market Value* on the sale of each piece of your *Personal Property* is akin to always selling your stocks at peak value…it just doesn't happen. We typically suggest to our clients that although they have the right to expect *Market Value* on the best-of-the-best of their items, they should strive to achieve *Orderly Liquidation Value*, which can provide them with *the greatest return…with the least amount of work…in the shortest amount of time.*

Do you still think that all "*Values*" are the same?

* * * * * * * * * *

Home Downsizing Tips

✓ Most *Personal Property* items will be sold in a *Secondary Market* situation, as-is, without warranty or guarantee, for a fraction of what you originally paid for it. Be prepared to accept this as fact because it will without doubt happen.

✓ Be wary of values received at Appraisal Fairs and Antique Road Show-type events. The knowledge of the "*Qualified Appraisers*" can vary widely, and verbal appraisals are often worth about as much as the puff of wind. Consider most of these verbal appraisals as nothing more than a starting point for further research into the true value of what you have.

✓ A Free Appraisal is usually worth as much as you have paid for it.

✓ If someone suggests to you a value that sounds too good to be true, ask them if they are willing to pay you that "*appraised value*"...*today*. Then watch how quickly they shy away from that number.

✓ Written Appraisals, completed in compliance with USPAP (*Uniform Standards, Professional Appraisal Practice*), are typically the best appraisals you can receive. Although a USPAP compliant Appraisal will cost you an appraisal fee, USPSP appraisers must follow a strict code of appraisal guidelines and ethics that insure that that you will receive an appraised value that is fair, honest, well researched, and un-biased.

✓ Insurance *Replacement Value* appraisals play an important role in our society. However, understand that in the vast majority of instances the amount you will be able to sell your *Personal Property* for will be far below the value listed in your "*Insurance Replacement Value*" appraisal. I can almost guarantee it.

✓ More often than not, in the real world your Personal Property will sell for an "*Orderly Liquidation Value*" rather than a "*Retail Value*". Be ready for this.

The best book we have ever seen that discussed "*Value*" is "*Appraising Personal Property: Principles and Methodology*" by David J. Maloney, Jr. (2nd Edition, 2007-2008). We studied this book extensively when studying for our *GPPA* and *15-Hour USPAP* Courses. This book offered the most in-depth discussion of value that we have ever seen and we would highly recommend it to anyone wishing to delve further into this subject.

If You Need An Appraisal: If you require a formal, written appraisal for estate, insurance, divorce, or any other legal purposes, we can help you in this area. We have earned both our *GPPA (Graduate Personal Property Appraiser)* and *MPPA (Master Personal Property Appraiser)* designations, and are *USPAP*-certified by the *Appraisal Institute* as well. Although USPAP appraisals will generally take longer and cost more, they will provide authentication as well as significantly more detail and accuracy.

Chapter 7

How and Where To Research Value

 Your primary objective now is to determine the value of your *Personal Property*? What's it really worth in today's market? How do you go about researching value?

I'll tell you here and now that it is extremely difficult for most individuals to determine a realistic current market value on each item in an entire house by yourself. Most people will need a *Professional In-Home Personal Property Walk-Through Valuation* or the help of a certified appraiser or an individual who has considerable experience in valuing *Personal Property*. And this will cost you money on the front end. It is not uncommon for professional appraisers to charge you $100-$200 per hour for their appraisal services.

And most of them are worth it. What are you getting in exchange for their valuation or appraisal fee?
- Access to their many years of *Personal Property* expertise.
- Access to the knowledge contained in their extensive reference libraries.
- Access to their knowledge of where to research items on the Internet.
- Access to their ability to work as *"Appraisal Detectives"* helping to locate realistic values comparable to the items that you have.
- You can receive an opinion of value on almost any item you request.
- You will receive an appraisal report, on their letterhead, that is good for legal, estate, divorce, tax or other purposes.

So, in exchange for what will probably amount to a few hundred dollars, you can have a professional tell you what your lifetime's collection of *Personal Property* is worth. Considering what you probably paid for it all, it seems like a very reasonable investment to me. (Do you remember the story of the $10,000 diamond ring being sold for $10, because the owners thought it was costume jewelry? They failed to bring in an outside expert.).

But for those interested in trying to do it yourself, in this chapter we'll introduce you to a variety of 16 resources and techniques that will enable you to do some value research on your own. This chapter will include eleven sources of *Free Value Information* that are available to you, as well as five sources of *Fee Value Information* that will cost you to access.

Free Value Information Sources
- eBay Completed Sales
- Search Engines
- Free Internet Sites
- Free Price Guides
- Free Trade Papers
- Free Appraisals by Friends
- Free Auction House Appraisals and Pre-Auction Estimates
- Retail Asking & Selling Prices
- Live Auctions
- Internet Malls and Stores

- Collector Clubs

<u>*Fee Value Information Sources*</u>
- Latest Price Guides
- Subscription Trade Papers
- Maloney's Antiques & Collectibles Resource Guide
- Fee Internet Sites
- Paid USPAP Appraisals

Free Value Information Sources

<u>***eBay Completed Sales***</u>: One of the easiest and fastest ways to determine what items are selling for today is to check the "*Completed Items*" category on eBay. This will tell you exactly what something has "*sold for*" on eBay within the past two weeks.

How do you do this?
- Go to: www.ebay.com
- In the "*Search*" box key in what you are looking for, such as "*Roseville Pine Cone 14"* *Vase*". This will take you to all of the "*Roseville Pine Cone 14" Vases*" that are up for sale on eBay today.
- However, this doesn't do you much good because these are incomplete transactions.
- On this same page you then want to go to the box on the left side marked "*Search Options*", scroll down and check the "*Completed Items*" box, and then click the "*Show Items*" button. This will list all "*Roseville Pine Cone 14" Vases*" that have sold within the past two weeks.

But don't be misled by this data because you will probably see a variation in the Completed Auction prices. This will has to do with factors such as:
- *Condition*
- Shipping Costs
- *Condition*
- Reputation of the Seller
- *Condition*
- Other factors.

But at least this is a starting place for determining the level of desirability for what you have.

There are three other important factors to look at while you are on this eBay page:
1. *The number of similar items listed.* If there are a fair number of other similar items, it could be a good sign indicating a reasonable level of interest in this category.
2. *The number of bids on each item.* A high number of bids suggests a high level of interest in this category. If there are relatively few bids in this category, it could suggest a low level of interest.
3. *The number of "Completed Sales" versus "No Sales".* A high number of "*No Sales*" or "*Incomplete Sales*" suggests a low level of interest in this category.

In summary one of the easiest ways to determine a ballpark value on many items today is to check eBay's *"Completed Sales"*, looking for *Price Level, Number of Bids*, and *Percentage of Completed Sales.*

Search Engines: Let's get this *Free Value Information Search Tool* out of the way quickly because it is so obvious. One of the first things you should do, probably even before seeking out any *eBay Completed Sales Values*, is to try a *Google Search.*

Another of my favorite *Search Engines* is www.dogpile.com *Dogpile* searches multiple Search Engines simultaneously, and returns the search results from all sites back to you in a single listing.

If at first you can't locate what you are searching for, try changing the wording of your search criteria. If you can't locate what you are looking for in these two Search Engines, you'll probably have a tough time finding it anywhere. But you should also try your other personal favorite Search Engines as well. There are thousands of Search Engines available, with most having some specific area of specialty. You may have luck elsewhere.

Free Internet Sites: Invariably your *Search Engine* searches will lead you to a wide variety of Web Sites. Some will be extremely helpful; most will not. Once you find a helpful Web Site, be sure to *Bookmark* it because you will probably want to return to it at some future date.

Some of my favorite free value-related web sites are:
- eBay   www.eBay.com
- Live Auctioneers   www.LiveAuctioneers.com
- Sotheby's   www.Sothebys.com
- Christie's   www.Christies.com
- Heritage Auctions   www.ha.com

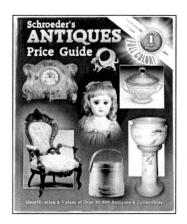

Free Price Guides: All price guides cost money, at least when they are originally sold. *"Free"* price guides, such as those you might access in the local library, are not necessarily bad. The problem with *"Free"* price guides is that they are usually outdated. Between 1980-today, tens-of-thousands of price guides and reference books have been published. Generally price guides come in two formats.

General Price Guides: *General Price Guides* are larger books (often 600+ pages) that feature values on a huge variety of Antiques and Collectibles categories. The publishers of these price guides closely follow and gather prices from a wide variety of sources including *Auctions, Antique Shops, Trade Papers*, etc.

51

They also make arrangements with specialists around the country who contribute representative pricing in their areas of specialty as well.

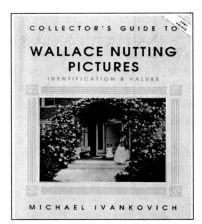

Specialty Price Guides: During the past 30 years the *Specialty Price Guide* was also introduced. Nearly every collectible category had its own individual price guide, and often there were competing price guides, printed by different publishers, and written by competing specialist authors. I have personally authored more than ten different editions of *Specialty Price Guides*.

Both types of price guides offer valuable background and reference information, as well as pricing and value data. When using a price guide, be certain to get the latest publication date possible. Although the background and reference information rarely goes out of date, the prices may no longer be accurate After many years of increasing prices during the 1980's-1990's, over the past five years prices have been declining in many categories. So if you use a price guide that is more than a few years old, although the background information should prove helpful, don't put too much faith in the prices.

Free Trade Papers: Antiques & Collectibles trade papers are published in all regions throughout the entire country, and many are distributed for free at places such as Auction Houses, Antique Shops, and Antique Shows.

The typical free Antiques & Collectibles publications will include local or regional information about the trade, and will usually include information such as:
- Antiques & Collectibles-related information and reference articles.
- Current trade events.
- Paid advertisements for Auctions, Antique Shows, and Antique Shops.
- Classified Buying & Selling Ads.
- Other items of interest.

These are not necessarily the best source for value information because they will require considerable work on your part, but they're free.

Free Appraisals by Friends: *"You get what you pay for"*. Occasionally you may receive a fair and honest appraisal from someone you know for free. But more often than not you will receive well-intended but erroneous value information when you seek *"Free"* appraisals.

There is nothing wrong with seeking free value information. You would be remiss if you didn't. However, when someone gives you a free opinion of value, don't necessarily accept that value as fact. Seek some additional confirming information by asking questions like:
- How did you arrive at that value?
- Is that value a guess, or can you confirm it?
- Is that value based upon today's world, or is it based on price levels from 5-10 years ago?

- Can I receive this value if I sell it on eBay or anywhere else today?

Free Auction House Appraisals and Pre-Auction Estimates: Many Auction Houses hold *Free Appraisal Days*. Customers are encouraged to bring in a limited number of items, typically only 1-2 items, for a "*Free Appraisal*". If you can locate a *Free Appraisal Day* in your area, you may want to consider taking 1-2 of your best items there for a "*Free Appraisal*".

Typically what you will receive is an Auctioneer's verbal opinion of value, That is, the Auctioneer will provide you with their opinion of what the item may sell for at their Auction. If you like the number, you can consign that item to one of their future Auctions. If you don't want to consign that item to Auction, you can take it home with you without fee or obligation. Beware of those Auctioneers who may inflate their appraised value in an attempt to induce you to consign it to their Auction.

Another problem with these is that you are limited to only a few items per session, so it would take quite some time to evaluate all of your items in this manner.

Retail Asking & Selling Prices: If you want to get a feel for what your items may be selling for in today's market, visit Antique Shops, Flea Markets, and Antique Shows to see what experienced dealers are *asking* for their merchandise.

We say "*asking*" because you must keep in mind that their "*asking price*" will not necessarily be their "*selling price*", and it will not necessarily be the price that you will receive for yours.
- As long as the dealer still has the merchandise, it remains unsold.
- Dealers will typically negotiate on price, so their final selling price is almost always lower than their asking price.
- Some dealers use lower asking prices in order to turn-over their merchandise more quickly; other dealers use higher asking prices in order to make the maximum profit on each item that they sell. Unless you know value, how will you differentiate between the high price and low price dealer?

And don't forget that the dealer asking price rarely has any direct connection to what they paid for the item. However, retail asking prices are another source of free pricing information.

Visit a Live Auction: If you want to really see what items are selling for today, visit a local Auction. As discussed in Chapter 6, Auctions represent an *Orderly Liquidation Market*, and you may be surprised at what you see. Some prices will be much higher than what you expect, while even more prices will probably be far less than you expected. However, in most instances Auction pricing represents true fair market value today because it represents fact, not someone's opinion. It represents what people are truly willing to pay for an item in the secondary market

Internet Malls and Stores: Over the past ten years many Antiques Dealers have gravitated from selling through traditional Antiques Shops and Shows, to selling through

Internet Antiques Stores and Malls. Whereas Internet Auctions use the *Auction Method of Selling*, Internet Stores and Malls use the more traditional *Retail Method of Selling*. Dealers list the merchandise in a Fixed Price format, where it will sit in the dealers store until it either sells or is removed by the dealer. You can purchase the item at the listed price, or you can negotiate via e-mail or telephone with the dealer to obtain a lower price.

Internet Malls and Stores, like the rest of the Internet is open 24/7/365. You can search for items within the malls & stores through a Search Function that is located within each Web Site.

Although there are many different Internet Antiques and Collectibles Malls and Stores, my three favorites are:
- *eBay Stores* at: www.ebay.com
- *The Internet Antique Store* at: www.tias.com
- *Collector Online* at: www.collectoronline.com

From a value perspective, you can access any of these Internet Malls, and key in whatever particular item you are seeking a value on. If you get a hit, it will show you a picture of the item that is for sale, and it will tell you what the dealer's asking price is. This can be helpful if you are trying to search ballpark values on particular Antiques & Collectibles.

Collectors Clubs: *Collectors Clubs* are organizations whose members specialize in collecting particular Antiques & Collectibles. For example, I have been a member of the *Wallace Nutting Collectors Club* for nearly 35 years. We collect Wallace Nutting pictures, books, furniture, and pretty much anything related to Wallace Nutting.

Many Collectors Clubs have web sites, hold annual conventions, publish e-mail and traditional hard-copy newsletters, and sometimes even publish the names and addresses of their members (although this is becoming less common due to privacy issues). If you have a particular Antique or Collectible that you are seeking to value or sell, you may want to try this route.

Two great sources for locating Collectors Clubs are:
- *The Association of Collecting Clubs*: www.collectors.org
- *Collectors Online*: www.collectoronline.com

Between these two Web Sites you will be able to access literally thousands of Collectors Clubs from around the world.

* * * * * * * * * *

54

Fee Value Information Sources

You get what you pay for. Although most people will gravitate first to the *Free Value* tools, the *Fee Value* tools will generally provide you with more current and accurate value information as well as save you time.

New Price Guides & Reference Books. The reason I also placed price guides and reference books under the "*Fee Value Information*" section as well as the "*Free Value Information*" section is that in order to obtain the most current pricing, you will need the most recently published price guide, and in order to locate it you may have to pay for it. We already covered some general information about price guides so I will not repeat that here.

For free value information you can always go to your local library. But in most cases the price guides you will find in your local library will be out-dated. There are so many different price guides in print that no library can afford to update theirs every year. And if you inadvertently use an outdated price guide, it could potentially cost you big money.

So if you have items that may have considerable value, if would probably be to your advantage to invest in the most current price guide possible in order to access the most current pricing possible.

Subscription Trade Papers & Publications: Although many Antiques & Collectibles trade papers and publications are provided for free by their publishers at Auctions, Antique Shops, and Antiques Shows, you will have to pay for the better ones.

One of my favorite is the *Maine Antiques Digest*. (www.maineantiquedigest.com). Published for more than 30 years *MAD* is the pulse of the higher-end Antiques & Collectibles market. It is published monthly, and it's 150+ pages per month covers the high-end Auction and Antiques Show market, including:
- Results at major national and international Auctions.
- Coverage of major national and international Antique Shows.
- What's happening in the market today.
- Hundreds of pictures & prices in each issue.
- Advertising by many of the country's leading dealers.

Although the advertising usually doesn't include asking prices, it will provide you will access to many of the country's leading specialty dealers, their store or web site addresses, and how to reach them in the event that you may be selling something that they may be interested in. However, *MAD* generally only covers the high-end Antiques market. If you are seeking information in other markets, you will have to look elsewhere.

Maloney's Antiques & Collectibles Resource Guide: Another excellent resource guide is *Maloney's Antiques & Collectibles Resource Directory*. It's a "*Fee*" book if you must buy it, or it can be a "*Free*" book if you can locate a copy in your Public Library or elsewhere. Published by David Maloney Jr., this book isn't necessarily a price guide, but rather a resource guide to the entire Antiques & Collectibles business. We have the 7th edition (the latest edition as we go to press with this book) in our library and its 862 pages are absolutely full of information about where you can get information about...and sell...almost any type of Antiques & Collectibles. You may even be able to locate this book in your local library.

This book is broken down into more than 1,000 specific collecting categories, with each collecting category including contact information for:
- Experts
- Appraisers
- Leading Collectors
- Clubs & Associations
- Periodicals
- Museums
- Libraries
- Other known information about each specialty category.

It also includes:
- Regional and national trade publication listings
- Repair & conservation contacts
- Much more.

The 7th edition was published in 2003 so don't expect this book to be 100% current or accurate because so much has changed in the market since then. But we are unaware of any other single publication that includes as much information as this book.

Fee Internet Research Sites:
Fee Internet research sites are larger, professionally compiled and maintained sources of valuable information about Antiques, Collectibles, and other related items. Some of these sites are *general* sites, which mean that they cover an extremely wide variety of items. Other sites are *specialized* sites, specializing in certain categories as Art, Sculptures, etc.

The primary advantage of *Fee Internet Research Sites* is that they will enable you to locate accurate information more quickly. These sites will enable you to:
- Identify your merchandise by viewing photos of similar items.
- Help determine current value by understanding what other comparable items are selling for.
- Help you to determine maker or artist.
- Help you to identify an illegible signature or unknown marking.
- View items that are similar to yours and currently for sale.
- Possibly even locate a selling venue for your items.

Two of my favorite Fee General Web Sites are:
- *Prices for Antiques*:   www.P4A.com
- *Price Miner*:   www.PriceMiner.com

Several of my favorite Fee Art-related sites are:
- *Ask Art*:   www.AskArt.com
- *Art Fact*:   www.ArtFact.com

- *Art Net*:   www.ArtNet.com
- *Art Price*:   www.ArtPrice.com
- *Gordon's Art*:   www.Gordonsart.com

Paid Appraisals

Written Appraisals, completed in compliance with *USPAP* (*Uniform Standards, Professional Appraisal Practice*), are typically the best appraisals you can receive. Although they will cost you an appraisal fee, *USPSP* appraisers much follow a strict code of appraisal guidelines that insure you will receive an appraised value that is fair, honest, accurate, and un-biased. When looking to have a formal appraisal done, be sure to seek out a *USPAP* certified appraiser.

Home Downsizing Tips

✓ When you are researching value, there are both Free and Fee Value Reference Tools available to you. The Free tools will save you money. The Fee tools will contain more current and accurate information as well as save you time. Use both to help determine what your *Personal Property* is worth.

✓ The Internet is without a doubt the best tool for researching value available to you today.

✓ Prices Guides are also valuable reference tools. The text and content found in price guides will rarely go out of date. However, prices in many categories have changed dramatically over the past 5-10 years so be sure to use the most recent price guide available to you.

✓ There will generally be a big difference between a retail asking price that you see in your travels, and what you will be able to sell your *Personal Property* for, because retail prices not only include what the dealer paid for the item, but also a share of the dealer's expenses, room to negotiate downward, and anticipated profit.

✓ When you are visiting an Antique Show, Antique Shop, or other such retail establishment, and see something similar to yours, assume that the value of your merchandise is worth no more than 50% of that dealer's asking price. Most dealers try to work on a 100% mark-up on their purchase price. And out of that 100% mark-up they must pay booth or show rents, travel expenses, gas, business administrative expenses…and still make a profit.

✓ An excellent source of potential buyers could be a Collectors Club who collects what you are selling.

✓ You get what you pay for. A paid appraisal from a USPAP certified appraiser will be more accurate than a free appraisal from a well-intended friend or family member 99.9% of the time.

✓ For current value information, use the latest possible Price Guides. If you have a substantial investment within a certain specialty, buy the latest Price Guide on the subject. If you use an outdated Price Guide, you will not be seeing current market values which could cost you big money when you sell.

In-Home Personal Property Valuations: Before selling anything, most individuals should have some form of valuation done of their Personal Property. An *In-Home Personal Property Walk-Through Valuation* is where a knowledgeable Personal Property Professional walks through your home and provides you with a ballpark estimate of what your Personal Property may be worth in today's market. If you live in our general area, we can do this for you. If we see any hidden treasures, we will tell you, and we can even list them for you on eBay. This is probably the fastest and least expensive way to learn the value of your Personal Property in today's rapidly changing market. For further details you can visit our Web Site: www.HomeDownsizingConsultants.com

---

AVID Step #2 Summary

This is the end of *AVID Step #2*. Between Chapters 5-7 our objective was to help you understand the value of your *Personal Property*. In these chapters:

✓ We introduced you to the Mathematics of Selling *Personal Property*.

✓ We introduced you to the many forms of "*Value*" in today's market.

✓ We explained why it is so important to obtain ballpark values on your *Personal Property* prior to selling anything.

✓ We showed you how you can try to value your *Personal Property* by yourself.

✓ A *Professional In-Home Personal Property Walk-Through Valuation* by a qualified individual will generally be better that attempting to do it yourself, and is the absolute minimum that you should do prior to selling anything.

✓ A *USPAP-complaint Appraisal* will generally be the best form of appraisal that you can obtain.

Now let's move on to *AVID Step #3* where we'll *Investigate 10 Selling and Disposition Options* that are available to you.

And then in *AVID Step #4* we'll discuss how you can *Dispose of All Excess Items* by creating a *Plan of Action*, and then *Executing* that *Plan of Action*.

AVID Home Downsizing System Step #3

Investigating Your Selling & Disposition Options

You have more selling options than you may realize, and you should use them to your advantage. In Chapters 8-17 we'll review:

✓ *10 Selling and Disposition Options Available To You*: There are no real surprises here, but we are going to cover a wide variety of options that are available to you when it comes time to dispose of your *Personal Property*. Rarely will all 10 selling options apply to a single situation. But the beauty of these is that they are like a *"buffet of selling options"* that allow you to pick and choose those options that feel right for you.

✓ *The Advantages and Disadvantages of Each Selling Option*: Each selling option has both advantages...and disadvantages. We'll help you to understand what these are...before you select any single one to begin selling your *Personal Property*.

*   *   *   *   *

How To Use This Section

Chapters 8-17 discuss ten different selling and disposition options that are available to you. Since you most likely won't be using all ten options, you don't necessarily need to read each chapter to benefit from this section. We would suggest that you only read those chapters that cover options you may be interested in using. For example, if you have absolutely no interest in selling through Antique Shops or Antique Shows, you don't really need to read those chapters (although we hope that you do).

So although we recognize that you may have no interest in certain of these options, we have included all ten options, along with the advantages and disadvantages of each, in order to help some of you decide whether these options may be right for you.

Chapter 8

Garage Sales: Perhaps the Worst Option of All

Have you ever conducted a Garage Sale? Most people have. And even if you never ran a Garage Sale before, almost everyone has attended a Garage Sale at some point in their lives. Some people love running Garage Sales. They love the personal interaction, the thrill of the unknown. The fun of stuffing cash into their pockets as people take away items that they no longer want or need.

Garage Sales are meant to be fun. You simply open up your garage to display your merchandise to potential customers. And if you don't have a garage, you can set-up on your driveway, your front lawn, around your house, or even inside your house. You simply advertise your Garage Sale, and invite people to come and purchase your merchandise. You set a price on each piece and then try to sell it.

Although Garage Sales can be fun for some people, running a Garage Sale is not for everyone. The major advantages of holding a Garage Sale are that they can be fun, and they allow you to liquidate merchandise with probably the least amount of expense. And you can do it with your family or friends.

Pricing Errors: Garage Sales also have disadvantages as well. Perhaps the greatest downside is that most people don't understand how to properly price things. If you don't understand value, you will inevitably overprice some things, and under-price other things. Which means that you may end up selling your more valuable items at far below market value.

As mentioned earlier, perhaps the saddest story I heard was the family who sold a $10,000 18k diamond ring for $10...because they didn't realize that Grandma's ring was real. Their mistake was that they didn't seek outside help. They priced everything themselves.

Early Birds: This pricing error problem leads to what's commonly called in the Garage Sale business as the "*Early Bird*". *Early Birds* are generally Antiques Dealers who know, for a fact, that most people running Garage Sales don't understand how to properly price their merchandise. *Early Birds* want to be the first person at a Garage Sale so they can purchase anything that the seller has under-priced. They will never buy things that are priced correctly, or over-priced.

If you advertise a Garage Sale for Saturday, expect the *Early Birds* to start knocking on

your door by Friday, or Thursday, or even as early as Wednesday afternoon. *Early Birds* usually try to hide the reason they are arriving early (which is to purchase all of your pricing mistakes) by offering some lame story, such as:

- *"I thought the Garage Sale was today. But as long as I am here, can I look?"*
- *"I can't make it this weekend because I'm working at my church, and it looks like you have some things I've been looking for."*
- *"I'm going into the hospital tomorrow for surgery and didn't want to miss your sale."*

Some Garage Sale owners actually like *Early Birds*...because they spend money. Some naïve people think that it was very nice of the *Early Bird* to purchase $300 worth of items. They consider this a very successful day. What they don't understand is that the *Early Bird* may have just walked away with $2500 of merchandise that was under-priced.

Time Commitment: The time commitment needed to run a Garage Sale is another major consideration. You don't simply have a Garage Sale that is successful. It takes considerable time to prepare, research pricing, set-up the event, run the sale, and then clean-up. A typical Garage Sale schedule may go something like this, and will depend upon the amount of merchandise that you have to sell.

- Tuesday: *5 hours*...to gather merchandise from your basement, attic, crawl space, upstairs in the garage, out-buildings, barns, or storage lockers.
- Wednesday: *5 hours*...to wash, dust, clean, and generally get the merchandise ready for the sale.
- Thursday: *5 hours*...to put price stickers on everything, ask around and check Price Guides for pricing, etc.
- Friday: *5 hours*...Begin setting up the sale.
- Saturday: *8 hours*...Begin setting up the outdoor merchandise from 6:00-7:00 AM, run the Garage Sale from 7:00 AM - 2:00 PM, and put merchandise back into the garage from 2:00-3:00 PM.

In this scenario, you've already logged in 28 hours running this Garage Sale, but at least you're done, right?

Wrong. In a typical Garage Sale you will only sell perhaps 10-20% of your merchandise. And what you do sell is usually the best and most desirable merchandise. Now, what do you do with what's left? No respectable Auctioneer or Antiques Dealer wants what's left after a Garage Sale. Your options are limited, and they will cost you either more hours of labor, or will eat into what you have made at your Garage Sale. Your options are:

- *Hold another weekend Garage Sale*. But that means more hours of labor, and subsequent Garage Sales are rarely as successful as the first.
- *Send it to Auction*. But no serious Auctioneer wants Garage Sale leftovers.
- *Sell it to an Antiques Dealer*. No serious Antiques Dealer wants Garage Sale leftovers either.
- *Bring in a Cleanout Specialist*. After a Garage Sale, *Cleanout Specialists* (See Chapter 22) will probably charge you to take it away, eating into the money you initially made at your Garage Sale.
- *Donate it to a Local Non-Profit*. But even non-profits and thrift stores are getting more selective, and will most likely take only the best of what's left, still leaving you with the real junk.

- *Bring in a Dumpster*. This is your final solution. And it will cost you.

Now, add up the hours you just spent disposing of the remaining merchandise. Just to make the math easy let's say 22 hours of labor. And now add those hours to the number of hours you spent running the initial Garage Sale. That will give you the total number of hours you have spent (wasted?) on running a Garage Sale. In this case 50 total hours.

Here is the *Net Garage Sale Return* formula that you can apply, assuming you made $500 or $1,000 at your Garage Sale.

Gross Revenue at Garage Sale:	$500	$1000
Less Advertising, Supplies & Other Expenses	$100	$ 100
Net Revenue from Garage Sale	$400	$ 900
Less Cost of Dumpster	$300	$ 300
Cash in Hand When Done	$100	$ 600
Divided by the Total Hours Worked (e.g., 50 hours) Net Hourly Wage	$2/hour	$12/hour

If two of you worked on the Garage Sale, divide this hourly wage in half. And this doesn't take into account what you may have paid for the merchandise.

I think you get the idea. Although some people love running Garage Sales, and whereas Garage Sales are the perfect option for some, when you look at the amount of work involved, for many individuals Garage Sales may perhaps be the worst option of all.

Garage Sale Advantages
- The ability to work at home.
- There is very little expense.
- It can be fun for some.
- It is mainly a cash business.
- You can dispose of items you no longer want or need.
- It's a great way to dump low-end items.
- You can do it with family and friends.

Garage Sale Disadvantages
- The general lack of understanding of the true value of most items.
- The ability to give things away for a fraction of their true value.
- People you don't know will be coming to your home.

- The time commitment involved with preparing for and conducting the actual sale can be significant.
- Items are sometimes stolen when your back is turned.
- What do you do with the unsold items, which is usually 80-90% of what you started with?

Garage Sale Summary: Garage Sales can be an excellent option for selling middle market merchandise to a limited number of people, in a low cost setting, that you control. Garage Sales are better suited for selling low-to-middle end merchandise rather than higher end merchandise, because Garage Sale attendees are notoriously cheap. The greatest downsides are your probable pricing mistakes, the time commitment required, and what to do with all of the merchandise that is left after the Garage Sale has ended.

Home Downsizing Tips

✓ Check with your local government to determine if you need a permit or license.

✓ See if friends and neighbors want to participate and have a *"Neighborhood Sale"* to attract more visitors.

✓ Hold your Garage Sale on the weekend when the traffic will be the highest.

✓ When possible, hold you Garage Sale when the weather is mild and dry.

✓ If time permits, make it a two-day Saturday-Sunday event, but recognizing that you will normally sell more on Saturday than Sunday.

✓ Advertise both in free classified papers and in the *Garage Sale* section of your local newspaper, featuring your best or most unusual items. Garage Sale ads are cheap and they will bring in the customers.

✓ Take advantage of any free advertising in your community i.e. supermarket bulletin boards, local business window signage, etc.

✓ Put up your Garage Sale signs 1-2 days before the actual sale.

✓ In some rural areas you can have your sale announced for free by a local radio station.

✓ Put up directional signs and balloons at major intersections. Be sure to include the date and address on the Garage Sale sign.

✓ Price items ahead of time and price everything with removable stickers or string tags. Remember that yard sales attract bargain hunters, so don't expect to sell anything of significant value this way.

✓ Be reasonable in your pricing. Remember that you are downsizing and you don't need the items any more.

✓ Check items before the sale to be sure you haven't included something you want by mistake.

✓ Display everything neatly and individually so customers don't have to dig through boxes.

✓ Have an electrical outlet so buyers can test appliances.

✓ Have plenty of bags and newspaper for wrapping fragile items.

✓ Get enough change, and keep a close eye on your cash.

✓ Don't accept checks unless you're well acquainted with the buyer.

✓ Start early, at 7:00-8:00 AM. Most serious Garage Sale attendees are done by 9:00-10:00 AM and if you miss them, you will miss out on the cash that they are looking to spend.

✓ Get enough people to help. Make sure your helpers arrive on time. Your biggest rush will be at the start of the sale and your help will do you little good after the initial rush has passed.

✓ If having a Garage Sale and you are interested in dumping it all, put up a sign indicating that complete buyout offers will be considered.

✓ Expect a larger crowd of bargain hunters early, then stragglers for a few hours, and then another rush towards closing time. These are the very experienced Garage Sale attendees who know that prices drop at the end of the day.

✓ Recognize that most Garage Sale attendees are bargain hunters and opportunity seekers. If you recognize this, you will be one step ahead of them.

✓ Rarely will you sell an expensive item at a Garage Sale, unless it is grossly underpriced.

✓ Consider what items might be of no use to you in your new home. Will you need that snow-blower in Florida? Dump it now.

✓ Donate post-sale leftovers to charitable organizations. Some will send a truck to your home to pick up the goods (be sure to get a receipt, as your donation may be tax-deductible). If you're turned down, it may be time to simplify things by throwing out the items in question.

Chapter 9

Tag Sales Are Different Than Garage Sales

Many people think that a *Tag Sale* and a *Garage Sale* are the same thing, but actually there is a very fundamental and important difference. A *Garage Sale* is run by the individual who owns the merchandise. With a *Tag Sale*, the individual who owns the merchandise *hires someone* more knowledgeable than them to run the actual sale.

A Tag Sale Professional generally has considerable product knowledge. They understand product. They understand quality. They understand the difference between Good-Better-Best. They understand what the current and local market will bear. And most importantly, they understand how to properly price most items, which helps to overcome the biggest short-coming of Garage Sales: *Accurate Pricing*. Most often Tag Sale Professionals are either Antiques Dealers or Appraisers, which is why they have the product knowledge.

In exchange for either a flat dollar amount, or a percentage of the gross sales, the Tag Sale Professional will come in and run the entire Tag Sale. The greater amount of work you ask them to do, the more they are entitled to charge you. They will clean and sort the merchandise, price it, and set up the entire sale. Once Tag Sale Day arrives, they deal with the customers. They will negotiate the fairest selling price, collect the money, and write up the receipts. After the Tag Sale has been completed the Tag Sale Professional will clean things up, and help you to dispose of the items that remain unsold. And most importantly, after the sale the Tag Sale Professional will provide you with detailed accounting of what things sold for, and after deducting their fee and related expenses, they will provide you with payment.

Expect the Tag Sale Professional to charge a commission of 25-35%...or more...depending upon the amount of work involved. And in addition to their selling commission, hourly fees may also apply to certain additional responsibilities that you delegate to them.

There are several advantages to Tag Sales. The primary advantage is that the Tag Sale Professional knows merchandise, and they know how to price it better than you, and they are less likely to "*give away*" merchandise than if you were pricing your own items. Other than that, the advantages of holding a Tag Sale are very similar to that of a Garage Sale.

There are also disadvantages to Tag Sales as well. There is a time commitment of usually several days of preparation time for the Tag Sale. You also incur advertising expenses. And probably the biggest disadvantage is that after the Tag Sale is over you are still left with a quantity of unsold merchandise. What do you do with that merchandise? After the better merchandise is gone, few people are interested in purchasing the remaining merchandise. But for some, a *Tag Sale* may be preferable to a *Garage Sale*, and at least you have the help of the *Tag Sale Professional.*

Tag Sale Advantages

- You can hire a Tag Sale Professional to do the work for you.
- You no longer have to be worried about knowing values (assuming that you have selected the proper person to run your Tag Sale).
- The ability to conduct the Tag Sale at your home.
- Although a nominal expense, it is still more expensive than a Garage Sale because you are now paying a second party to sell your excess merchandise.
- It can be fun for some.
- You can dispose of items you no longer want or need.
- It's a great way to dump low-end items.

Tag Sale Disadvantages
- The fee that you must pay to the Tag Sale Professional.
- It is no longer a cash business because the Tag Sale Professional will probably pay you with a check.
- People you don't know will still be coming to your home.
- The time commitment needed to prepare for and conduct the actual Tag Sale.
- Your home may be in a state of disarray for a week or more.
- What to do with the unsold items, which is usually 80-90% of what you started with?

Tag Sale Summary: Tag Sales can be an excellent option for selling middle market merchandise to a limited number of people, in a reasonably low cost setting, that you control through your Tag Sale Professional. Tag Sales are better suited for selling low-to-middle-end merchandise rather than higher-end merchandise, because Tag Sale attendees, like Garage Sale attendees, are bargain hunters, and as a group are opportunity seekers. A good Tag Sale Professional can be worth their weight in gold.

Home Downsizing Tips

✓ Most of the Garage Sale *Home Downsizing Tips* will also apply to Tag Sales.

✓ Referrals are usually to best way to locate a good Tag Sale Professional. The more good things you hear, the more likely they will do a good job for you.

✓ Be certain that the Tag Sale Professional you select is honest because if not, they can steal you blind.

✓ Make sure that your Tag Sale Professional notifies their customer mailing list about your sale.

✓ Once you hire a Tag Sale Professional, trust them and stay out of their way. Don't micro-manage them. You hired them because they were the best you were able to locate. Let them do their job of selling of your merchandise and stay out of their way.

Need A Speaker For Your Group or Organization?

Home Downsizing Seminars and Workshops: If you would like us to come to your group or organization and present either a one-hour Home Downsizing Seminar or a ½-Day Home Downsizing Workshop, contact us for further details, or visit our *Home Downsizing Workshop* Web Site. In many instances, distance factors can easily be resolved.
www.HomeDownsizingWorkshops.com

Chapter 10

Selling at a Flea Markets

If you prefer not to have the customers coming to your house (*Garage Sale* and *Tag Sale*), then you can go to where the customers go...*the Flea Market.*

According to *Wikipedia*, The first Flea Market is thought to have been the *Marché aux puces* of Saint-Ouen, Seine-Saint-Denis, in the northern suburbs of Paris. It is a large, long-established outdoor bazaar, one of four in Paris. They earned their name from the flea-infested clothing and rags sold there. From the late 17th century, the makeshift open-air market in the town of Saint-Ouen began as temporary stalls and benches among the fields and market gardens where rag-pickers exchanged their findings for a small sum.

Flea Markets have been an extremely popular buying and selling venue in the United States since the early 1970's, although they have been undergoing some radical changes over the past 5 years.

Basically there are four distinct types of Flea Markets:

- *Antique & Collectibles Flea Markets*: These are Flea Markets where only Antiques, Collectibles, or other similar items are allowed. These markets tend to attract serious buyers of Antiques & Collectibles because that is the primary commodity offered at such markets. Crafts, reproductions, and newer items have been either banned or frowned upon. Unfortunately, as the Antiques & Collectibles markets have softened over the past 5-10 years, Flea Market promoters have been forced to loosen their standards and accept more of these types of dealers, just to fill their table and booth capacities.

- *General Merchandise Flea Markets*: These are the type of Flea Markets that you will most commonly see around the country today. Although you may see an occasional Antique & Collectible dealer at these Flea Markets, you will see far more newer merchandise than anything else, including things such as household items, newer furniture, linens, jewelry, decorative items, tools, sporting goods, clothing, wallets & purses, records, tapes, CD's, & DVD's, etc. General Merchandise Flea Markets are often huge because of the wide variety of merchandise allowed, and hence the larger pool of potential dealers. Some items are hand-made crafts or otherwise unique items. The vast majority of items are brand new and frequently imported from Asia and elsewhere. It is quite common to see illegal knock-offs of major high-end name products (e.g., Rolex watches) being sold as original at these Flea Markets.

- *Specialty Product Flea Markets*: Not as common as the first two Flea Markets mentioned, you can sometimes find Specialty Flea Markets that sell a limited type of merchandise, and which are only trying to attract a specialty customer. Examples of these could include a Ski Club Flea Market where club members sell used skis and ski accessories to each other, or an Antique Radio Club that invites its members to buy and sell that specific commodity.

- *Household Item Flea Markets*: Although most prefer not to be referred to as such, that is basically what they are. Typically held on Saturdays by Churches, Firehouses, and other such non-profits, these are held as fund raisers by these groups. They place an advertising sign in front of their facility and a local classified ad for about a month prior, seeking to attract both vendors and buyers. They charge a nominal amount for table or space rent, spend a few dollars on advertising, and the profit goes into their general fund. Although you may occasionally see a few Antique & Collectible dealers set up at these events, the vast majority of merchandise being offered is general household merchandise, the type you would normally see at a Garage Sale, being sold by people attempting to downsize their homes. Sound familiar?

How Can You Sell At A Flea Market? First select a Flea Market to test. Probably one close to your home is better. If you enjoy the experience and make money, you can test the waters further away. Some Flea Markets allow you to just show up, take a table or space, and eventually management will come around and collect the booth rent from you. Most better Flea Markets are filled close to capacity, and the only way you will get a table is to call ahead and reserve. We would recommend that you always call ahead and reserve a booth.

Once dealer space has been secured, you treat it like your own little business. Table coverings will make you look more professional. You should price your merchandise ahead of time, because if this is your first time, you will inevitably attract *"The Pickers"*.

The Pickers: *Pickers* are quite a bit like the Garage Sale *"Early Birds"*. *Pickers* are professional buyers who travel extensively looking for things to buy and sell. More often than not *Pickers* don't even own a shop or set up at Antique Shows. They are an extremely independent, knowledgeable group who know merchandise well, can spot a bargain when they see it, and make a living at *"Buying Low, Selling for a Profit"*. Because their expenses are low (no shop rents, no booth fees), they are frequently willing to work on a smaller profit margin and would prefer to *"Flip"* an item for a smaller, short-term profit, rather than holding onto it for a longer period of time, tying up their money while waiting for a larger profit.

Anyway, on your first day selling at the Flea Market, be ready for *"The Pickers"* to descend upon you. They will smell you out, like a cat smelling a mouse. *Pickers* have been working each Flea Market for years, and they know the faces. If you have never sold at this market before, "*The Pickers*" will know it. And they will descend upon you. Be prepared for it. I can almost guarantee that it will happen.

Pickers are not looking for pots & pans, upholstered furniture, 8-track cassette tapes, or canning jars. Rather, *Pickers* are looking for valuable Antiques & Collectibles, things that you don't even know that you have: Sterling Silver, better named China & Glass, Gold Jewelry and Watches, Lionel Trains, signed Oil Paintings, and ten thousand other valuable items. If they see you unpacking the junk, they will depart fairly soon. If they see you unpacking better items, watch out. You will feel like you are a trader on the floor of the New York Stock Exchange.

Here's what you can expect from the *Pickers*:
- They'll begin holding your better items so the other Pickers cannot pick them up and buy them (Trust me, you won't get paid for a while yet).
- They'll start confusing you by asking you the price on un-priced items.
- They'll further confuse you by asking you if you can do better on that price (the price that you probably already forgot you quoted).
- Then they'll ask you for a pricing discount on multiple items.
- Some will try to help you unpack your boxes…trying to get into the better boxes before the other Pickers.
- And others will start slowly working their way to the backside of your table, trying to get a better look at what hasn't yet come out of your car or truck (again, trying to get to it before the other *Pickers*).

Sometimes you will have 10-20 pickers around you and trying to get your attention, all at once. If this happens, stop and reconsider what you are doing. If you have this many people trying to acquire your merchandise, you must have something good, and you probably have it priced too cheaply. The good news is that eventually the Pickers will leave you alone, but usually only after you have unpacked all of your merchandise. Or after you have been picked clean of anything of value.

The Crowd: The greatest advantage of selling at a Flea Market is the crowd. While you may see 50-100 people at a Garage Sale, perhaps 1000-2000 or more may walk past your booth at a Flea Market. Larger Flea Markets can attract crowds of 10,000+ on a single day, which certainly increases your chances of selling more merchandise.

The Downside of Selling at Flea Markets: The biggest problem with selling at Flea Markets is that now you are back to the Garage Sale issue: *Your lack of Value knowledge and pricing*. Your selling costs can also be greater than with a Garage Sale. And with a larger number of exhibitors, the competition will be greater.

And now you also have the added problem of having to box everything up, transporting it to the Flea Market, unpack it, and set it up in a sellable fashion on the table. After spending 8-

10 hours selling at the Flea Market, you must re-box all that didn't sell (usually the vast majority), put it back on the truck, take it home, unpack the truck, and start the process all over again the next week.

There indeed can be a considerable amount of additional work using of the Flea Market approach, but it does work for some people. I did it more many years when I was younger, and like it more than I disliked it.

But as with the Garage Sale option of selling, most likely at the end of the Flea Market process you will be left with a wide variety of merchandise, which is usually the least desirable and hardest to dispose of.

Flea Market Advantages
- There is a larger crowd of potential buyers.
- These buyers are generally at the Flea Market to spend money.
- The expense will be reasonable.
- It can be fun for some.
- It's mostly a cash business.
- It allows you to dispose of items you no longer want or need.

Flea Market Disadvantages
- Your probable lack of understanding of the true market value of items.
- The ability to give things away for a fraction of true worth.
- The time involved with preparing for and working the actual market.
- You must travel to the Flea Market.
- You will see increased competition from other dealers.
- Dealing with *Pickers*.
- Packing and unpacking…many times.
- The table and booth expense.
- You must carry tables, supplies, etc.
- You will most likely need a truck, van or station wagon.
- You must still dispose of the remaining items, which is usually 80-90% of what you started with.
- You must give up weekends to work most Flea Markets.

Flea Market Summary: For some, Flea Markets can be a great way to dispose of a larger amount of merchandise. Larger crowds who are there to spend money represent the #1 advantage of selling at Flea Markets. Disadvantages include the probability of mispricing items, higher expenses, travel time, increased competition, and the need to continually pack and unpack.

Home Downsizing Tips

✓ Recognize that all Flea Markets are not the same. Better markets attract better buyers (translation: *buyers who spend money*) and those are the markets you should set up in.

✓ Start early. At some markets a 5:00 AM start is the norm. Most serious buyers are done by 8:00-9:00 AM and are already moving on to another Flea Market or event. If you miss them, you will miss out on the cash that they are looking to spend.

✓ Recognize that early buyers are normally your more serious buyers and are there to spend money.

✓ Shoppers later in the day are typically *"Tire Kickers"* who rarely spend as much as the early buyers.

✓ Anticipate the *"Be Backs"*. *"Be Backs"* are people who show some interest in something in your booth, then leave and shop the rest of the show looking for better bargains. Before leaving your booth they often indicate that they may *"Be Back"* later. Often they never return. But sometimes they do, and *"Be Backs"* can be the difference between an okay show and a great show.

✓ A corner booth is normally worth the added expense because it provides you with more display space.

✓ See if a friend or neighbor is willing to share the booth (and work) with you.

✓ Most Flea Markets are held on the weekends, but there are also some very successful Flea Markets held on weekdays.

✓ You will generally sell better when the weather is mild and dry.

✓ A two-day Saturday-Sunday event will generally yield higher sales but present twice as much work and expense.

✓ Price items ahead of time and price everything with removable stickers or string tags.

✓ Be reasonable in your pricing. Remember that you are downsizing and you don't need the items any more.

✓ Be ready to negotiate. It's part of the Flea Market experience. (See Chapter 24 for more on Negotiation Techniques).

✓ Be ready for *"The Pickers"*.

✓ Display everything neatly and individually so customers don't have to dig through boxes.

✓ Have plenty of bags and newspaper for wrapping fragile items.

✓ Get enough change, and keep a close eye on your cash.

✓ Ask for cash. Don't accept checks unless you're well acquainted with the buyer.

✓ Bring food, coffee, water and snacks. Although most Flea Markets offer these, each trip that you must take can leave your booth un-attended. Save your few trips for bathroom breaks.

✓ Try to make friends with and get-along with your neighbors. Most are good people who typically rely upon each other to watch their booth when they must take a quick break.

✓ In colder weather wear layered clothing that can be shed as the day warms up.

Need A Speaker For Your Group or Organization?

Home Downsizing Seminars and Workshops: If you would like us to come to your group or organization and present either a one-hour Home Downsizing Seminar or a ½-Day Home Downsizing Workshop, contact us for further details, or visit our *Home Downsizing Workshop* Web Site. In many instances, distance factors can easily be resolved.
www.HomeDownsizingWorkshops.com

Chapter 11

Selling in Antique & Consignment Shops

Selling your Personal Property through Antique or Consignment Shops will be an option that relatively few people who are *Home Downsizing* will use and you may want to skip this entire chapter. But for some, especially those with a larger inventory of better Antiques & Collectibles, this might be a desirable option.

Basically there are three types of Antique Shops.

- *Individual Antiques Shops*: These are shops which are owned by a single individual, or sometimes a partnership between two or more individuals.

- *Group Antique Shops*: These are shops where the shop owner rents booth or display case space to Antiques Dealers who manage their own dealer space.

- *Consignment Antique Shops*: These are shops where individuals can bring in their merchandise and have the shop owner do all of the work in exchange for a higher commission.

Individual Antiques Shops

At the beginning of the collectibles craze in the early-mid 1970's, most Antique Shops were individually owned shops. They were usually situated in someone's home, garage, or barn. Most Antique Shops were single-owner shops. Some were partnerships, often among family or friends. Individual Antique Shops could be found in downtown business districts, on the country roadside, or in the home of, or on the property of, the individual shop owner. They were usually small, but intimate shops. They were often quaint and had character. You never knew

what you were going to find and there were almost always surprises in an Individual Antiques Shop.

The beauty of the Individual Antique Shop was the opportunity it presented to find bargains. No dealer knows everything and most individual shops had many under-priced collectible bargains just waiting to be found.

The primary advantage to owning an *Individual Antique Shop* is that the shop owner calls the shots. They set their own hours, work when they want to work, sell what they want to sell, and hope to make a profit.

The two greatest disadvantages are the time commitment and expense. Most Antiques business is done on weekends, which means that if you want to sell Antiques & Collectibles out of your own shop, you will most likely have to work weekends. This works for some, it doesn't work for others. If you are not willing to work weekends, either hire someone to staff your shop, or stay out of the Antiques business.

Rent may be your biggest expense. There is no rent if you work out of your home, which is why so many individual shop owners work at home. However, home-based Antique Shops usually mean fewer customers than shops located in more well-traveled areas. Shop rents can be quite expensive in certain areas, and may or may not be justified to attract the higher walk-in traffic. In this era of declining Antiques & Collectibles sales, we are seeing more Individual Antique Shops closing than opening.

Group Antique Shops

As the Antiques & Collectibles craze began to grow in the late 1970's-early 1980's, the *"Group Antiques Shop"* came into being. The Group Shop was basically a larger shop with an accumulation of multiple Antique Dealers, all under one roof. Several hundred dealers under a single roof was not uncommon. The Group Shop addressed the biggest problem associated with owning an individual shop: *the time commitment involved.* Although it was nice to operate an Antique Shop in your home or barn, the downside was that you had to be physically there in order for your shop to show a profit. If you were unable to work yourself, you typically had to pay someone to run your shop for you.

Beginning around 1980 the *Group Shop* changed all that...*for a small monthly fee.* The Group Shop was able to rent space to multiple Antique dealers, who would then stock their own shelves or square footage within their booth, with varying kinds of merchandise. The owners of the Group Shop would make money by collecting rents from the individual booth owners, and from this monthly revenue pay the monthly rent to the landlord, pay the advertising expense, pay the Group Shop staffing, pay all other business expenses, and any money left at the end of the month represented their profit.

There were many advantages to the Group Shop. Most shops were open 6-7 days per week, thereby giving dealers' merchandise significantly more exposure than it would have received in an individual shop. The more dealers in the shop, the broader the range merchandise.

The more dealers in a Group Shop, the better assortment and quality of merchandise, the farther shoppers would travel to get to that Group Shop. Few people would drive to too far off the beaten path to visit an unknown Individual Antiques Shop. But during the late-1970s, 1980s, and 1990s, it was not uncommon for collectors and dealers to establish regular antiquing routes throughout various regions and states, based primarily upon the location of the various Group Shops. I, for one, had a regular route that took me through New York State, into Massachusetts, through Vermont, into New Hampshire, back down through Massachusetts, into Connecticut, and back home to Pennsylvania, with the route based almost entirely upon the location of the specific Group Shops that I wanted to visit.

But there were disadvantages to the Group Shop concept as well. First of all, the pricing was more rigid, with generally only a maximum *"dealer discount"* of 10% being allowed off the listed price. Occasionally if you were willing to wait for an answer, some Group Shop staff were considerate enough to call the dealer with your offer, if your offer was both reasonable and firm. But more often than not the additional 5%-10% discount that you might receive on one $50-$100 item simply wasn't worth the additional wait. Conversely, if you were dealing with an Individual Shop owner, that owner was capable of providing you with an immediate *"Yes"*, *"No"*, or *"Counter-offer"* to your offer. Negotiating and haggling was often one of the best parts of buying Antiques.

Another major disadvantage of the Group Shop was that the best merchandise was usually picked over fairly quickly, either by shop employees, or Group Shop dealers who were in the shop servicing their booths. What usually happened was that immediately after a dealer re-stocked their booth with new merchandise, either the store employees or anyone else who was in the shop immediately checked things out, looking for under-priced inventory. As a result there were generally fewer bargains found in Group Shops as compared to Individual Antiques Shops. But Group Shops were still fun, there were a lot of them, and they offered an incredibly wide variety of merchandise, all in one single location.

Again the issues are still the same. You need to know how to price your merchandise. There is always merchandise left once the day is done. And it involves a considerable amount of work and time commitment.

Consignment Antique Shops

If you opt to sell your Antiques & Collectibles in an Antique Shop setting, perhaps the best option available to you may be a *"Consignment Shop"*. Sometimes the best *"Consignment Shop"* may be an *Individual Antiques Shop* in your home area, for others, a *Group Antiques Shop* may prove to be the best place to consign your merchandise.

The greatest advantage of the *Consignment Shop* is that you don't have to understand how to price your merchandise. You simply need to locate

76

a suitable *Consignment Shop*, take your merchandise to them, and they will do all of the work. They will price it, display it, sell it, collect the proceeds, and periodically send you a check. If an Antique Shop doesn't advertise that it accepts consignments, ask. Most shops are willing to accept quality consignments.

The greatest disadvantage is the cost. *Consignment Shops* will often charge you 25-50% of the final sale price, which at first glance may seem high. But when you understand what you are getting for that commission, it should appear much more reasonable, because:
- You are having a knowledgeable person price your merchandise.
- You are using their space.
- You are accessing their customer base.
- They handle all of the money.
- You pay no advertising.
- All you must do is drop off the merchandise and collect your check each month.

When all factors are considered, this should seem to be a very fair arrangement. And when compared against the options of opening your own *Individual Antiques Shop* or participating in a *Group Shop*, for many the *Consignment Shop* Option may be the best option of all.

HOME DOWNSIZING TIP: Remember that most Antique Shops are interested in purchasing items outright and privately. You may want to consider asking them what they would pay you for it all. If the price seems fair, you may want to accept their offer and be done with it, without paying a commission, without delay, and with a known amount of cash in hand.

Antique Shop Advantages
- There is a larger crowd of potential interested buyers.
- Antiques Shops are often open 6-7 days per week.
- The expense can be reasonable.
- It can be fun for some.
- You can dispose of items you no longer want or need.
- You can sell higher priced items than in the other options discussed so far.
- There is no time commitment in most Group or Consignment Shops.
- Some Group Shops will even allow you to offset your booth rent if you work a specific number of hours each month in the shop.

Antique Shop Disadvantages
- The time involved with servicing your booth.
- There is some travel involved.
- There is some packing and unpacking involved.
- With Individual Shops you must give up weekends.
- You may have to work some days in some Group Shops.
- What do you do with the items that fail to sell?
- Slower payment dates, perhaps only once or twice per month.

Antique Shop Summary: Selling through an Antique Shop will work for those who have better Antique & Collectible merchandise, and who have the inclination to sell in this venue. Although there is more work involved, if you have the right merchandise, the rewards can be significantly greater as well. Although this option works well with Antiques and Collectibles, it does not work as well with household items.

Home Downsizing Tips

✓ You will need the proper mix of Antiques & Collectibles in order to utilize this selling option.

✓ You will need a significant amount of merchandise to open an Individual Antique Shop. You can utilize the Group Shop and Consignment Shop options with considerably less merchandise.

✓ This option will allow you to sell higher-priced merchandise than with certain other selling options.

✓ There can be a major difference between Group Shops and Consignment Shops. Ownership, location, and quality of dealers can all have an impact on the volume of customer traffic, and hence on the volume of your sales. Select your Group or Consignment Shop wisely.

Chapter 12

Selling on the Antique Show Circuit

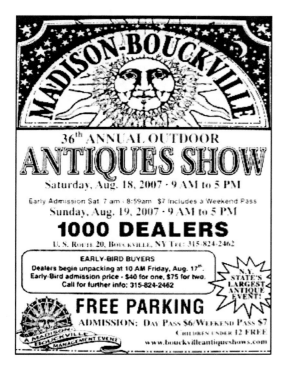

Selling your Personal Property at Antique Shows is probably the selling option that the fewest of you will take advantage of. Therefore, this will be a short chapter and if you have no interest in this method of selling, you may want to skip to the next chapter. We include it because this option offers several unique advantages not available in the other selling options. And we do know of people who have successfully made it work.

One couple we are familiar with were two professionals who had collected Antiques for more than 25 years. He was an executive and she was a schoolteacher. They worked hard Monday-Friday, and played hard on weekends, usually in pursuit of Antiques. They bought Antiques for years, traveling to Garage Sales, Flea Markets, Antique Shows and Antiques Shops, seeking out their favorite forms of collectibles. Even though their house was full, like most true collectors they continued buying.

As the time for retirement and downsizing approached they had a Garage Sale. But their merchandise was too good for a Garage Sale and nothing substantial sold. They tried selling at local and regional Flea Markets with the same results. They had the right merchandise, they knew what it was worth, and refused to give it away at below-market prices. They thought about selling at Auction, but decided to try one more thing before going that route. They had been attending Antiques Shows for years and always thought that they might like to become Antiques dealers some day. They understood how the business worked and they decided to try selling at Antique Shows in an attempt to bring their better Antiques & Collectibles to the retail market.

So they started their own professional Antiques business. They created a sole proprietorship with a professional Antiques-sounding name. They purchased tables, table draperies, and display cases with which they could more attractively display their merchandise. They knew several local show promoters and had no problem getting into local shows. They remained on the local show circuit for several years and, at least for these two individuals, the concept of selling their excess Personal Property at Antiques Shows worked.

The Earliest Antique Shows

Antique Shows are a relatively recent phenomenon. There were no known Antiques Shows in the 19th century because America's true collecting movement didn't even begin until circa 1910-1940. During this period of America's *Colonial Revival Movement*, collectors began actively pursuing colonial-era artifacts, including furniture, art, and decorative accessories.

It was during this period that American's first Antiques publications evolved, with first issue of the magazine "*Antiques*" being published in 1922. That magazine proved so popular with collectors that it is still being published today.

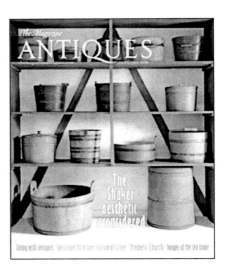

And it was during this 1910-1940 period that Antiques Shows began to appear. Reduced to its greatest simplicity, it takes three groups to conduct an Antique Show:

- *Sellers*...who have the merchandise to sell
- *Buyers*... who have an interest in acquiring that merchandise, and...
- *Show Promoters*...who know how to bring both groups together.

With America's growing collector base, Antiques Shows were a logical meeting place for buyers and sellers. Initially Antique Shows were a major annual event, typically in larger East Coast cities. Over time, as the collecting base continued to expand, once-a-year shows grew to multiple shows per year, with additional show promoters entering the mix. And slowly Antiques Shows began to expand into smaller cities and towns as well. By the late 1990's there were so many Antiques Shows that the market became over-saturated. But in the beginning, Antique Shows were a relatively uncommon event.

Today's Antiques Show Circuit

If you are considering exhibiting at Antiques Shows, you must understand that there are different levels of Antique Shows. You also need to understand that Show Promoters control the Antiques Show circuit, and they are the ones who set the tone of the show. Show Promoters determine which dealers are allowed to do a show, because better promoters understand that in order to succeed, they need the right mix of better sellers and buyers.

They need:
- Sellers who carry the best merchandise.
- Buyers who have the money and desire to purchase that merchandise.

Promoters understand that the money will follow the merchandise. Shows with the best dealers will attract the customers willing to buy the merchandise and having the means to do so. The more money that a particular dealer makes at a show, the more they will want to exhibit at that show again. If a dealer fails to make the necessary profit at a show, they most likely will not return, but will seek out another show with another promoter. Hence, good Show Promoters understand that in order for them to make money, they must help their dealers make money. And they do this by seeking out the best available dealers who, in turn, will attract the customers with the most money, and the willingness to spend that money on Antiques.

The Antiques Show circuit typically looks like this:

- *Flea Markets*: Many Antique Show dealers start out as *Flea Market* dealers. There are many participants at this level, but very few will make it too far up the Antiques Show circuit pyramid.
- *Small, Local Antiques Shows*: These are typically local, starter, or entry-level shows. They are relatively easy to get into. The level of merchandise is not all that high. The level of showmanship is certainly better than Flea Markets, but generally not all that fancy. These shows often have dealer tables only, but no walls.
- *Larger Local Antiques Shows*: These are generally better local shows. They have a strong local following, with primarily local or regional dealers. Buyers will probably travel no more than one hour to attend one of these shows. Some dealers in these shows can and do exhibit at better shows; others are aspiring to do better shows and are using this level show as a stepping stone to exhibiting at better shows. These shows often have pegboard or drapery walls.
- *Regional Antiques Shows*: These would include better regional shows, where both dealers and buyers will travel a longer distance to participate, the dealers because of the sales potential, and the buyers because of the quality and variety of merchandise to be found. Travel distances of 2 or 3 hours is not uncommon for buyers, perhaps longer for dealers if the show offers good sales potential. These represent better shows, with better dealers, and with a larger number of dealers, but they are certainly not national or international shows. Dealers at these shows can exhibit at any lower level show that they wish, but they would prefer to enter a higher level show whenever possible.
- *National Antiques Shows*: These would include major national shows, but just below the top national-international level. These shows include high-end, highly experienced dealers who, for whatever reason, are simply unable to make it into the international show level yet. They are typically making good money at this level, and could exhibit at any lower level that they wished, but they would prefer to enter the top level whenever possible. It is not uncommon for major buyers to fly to attend such national shows.
- *National-International Antiques Shows*: The major National and International Shows, which attract the best-of-the-best dealers, are the "*Major League*" of the show circuit. The promoters of these shows are extremely selective and they only select the finest dealers, with the best merchandise, good reputations, and a strong show followings. These shows always have long waiting lists to get in, and often the only way to get into such shows is if a dealer dies, or if an opening occurs because the promoter terminates the contract of a specific dealer, feeling that another particular dealer would be better for the show. It is not uncommon for major international buyers to fly to the U.S. to attend such shows.

Better shows will fill up quickly and usually have waiting lists. There is often competition among Antiques dealers to get into a better show. Show promoters will always ask dealers *"What shows have you done in the past?"* in an attempt to determine their level of experience and merchandise. And Antique Dealers will typically ask other dealers what shows they have done in an attempt to get a better understanding of their level on the Antique Show circuit pyramid.

What factors influence an Antique Show's attendance or gate?
- Quality of the dealers.
- Reputation of the promoter and his/her following.
- Location of the show.
- Accessibility and parking.
- Timing of the show.
- Weather.
- Price of admission.

Is this selling option right for you? Probably not. You need the right merchandise. You need the right image. It can be expensive to set up at an Antique Show, with booth rents running into the hundreds of dollars for local and regional shows, to many thousands of dollars to set up at the major national shows. You will need to give up your weekends, and you will have the same packing and unpacking problems. You still have the problem of pricing your merchandise, so you better understand values with higher-end merchandise. And as a new exhibitor, you will probably be limited to starting out at smaller local shows.

So the bottom line is that although the rewards for a few may be greater when selling at an Antique Show, the expenses are also higher and the Antique Show circuit is not for the faint of heart.

HOME DOWNSIZING TIP: For many, a better idea might be to consign your better Antique items to a qualified Antique Dealer who exhibits at better Antique Shows, and pay them a commission to sell your better Antiques in their booth.

Antique Show Advantages
- A larger crowd of potential buyers.
- The sales potential can be considerably greater than in the other selling venues.
- The buyers are generally more serious buyers if they have to pay to enter a show, versus a show that is free.
- It can be fun for some.
- It allows you to dispose of higher priced items than you could using certain other selling options.

Antique Show Disadvantages
- The expense can be considerably higher.
- The time commitment involved with preparing for and exhibiting at the show.
- The travel that may be involved.
- The packing and unpacking, multiple times, if you exhibit at multiple shows.
- You must give up weekends, because most Antiques Shows are on weekends.
- You must get into the "*right*" shows if you want to make good money.

Antique Show Summary: Selling in Antique Shows will work for those who have better Antique & Collectible merchandise, and who have the inclination to sell in this venue. Although there is more work involved and the expense can be higher than under other options, if you have the right merchandise, the financial rewards can be significantly greater as well.

Home Downsizing Tips

✓ Antique Shows are a relatively recent phenomenon.

✓ Very few people who are *Home Downsizing* will have any interest in selling their Personal Property on the Antiques Show circuit. However, for a few it may be one of the best alternatives, if you have the right merchandise.

✓ All Antique Shows are not the same. Different shows cater to different levels of dealers, and different levels of customers. Be sure to select a show that is suitable to what you have to sell.

✓ Today there are more Antiques Shows closing than opening, and many shows are having a difficult time locating quality dealers as more and more dealers are either leaving the business or gravitating to the Internet.

Need A Speaker For Your Group or Organization?

Home Downsizing Seminars and Workshops: If you would like us to come to your group or organization and present either a one-hour Home Downsizing Seminar or a ½-Day Home Downsizing Workshop, contact us for further details, or visit our *Home Downsizing Workshop* Web Site. In many instances, distance factors can easily be resolved.
www.HomeDownsizingWorkshops.com

Chapter 13

Sell It Yourself on eBay

In this chapter, whenever we refer to *"eBay"*, consider this to mean either selling on *"eBay"*, or anywhere else on the Internet.

eBay and the Internet have changed the way the world buys and sells Antiques, Collectibles, and most other commodities. It is barely 10 years old, yet it has become one of America's most successful businesses. There are more 200,000,000 registered eBay users, with nearly 100 million of them registered within the United States alone. It is reported that nearly 25% of the United States population has been involved in some type of eBay transaction. eBay makes somewhere around $4 billion a year, and they oversee more than $14 billion in various subsidiaries including PayPal, Skype, and other entities.

eBay has had a tremendous impact upon the Antiques and Collectibles business, and it has had a tremendous impact upon most other important buying and selling segments of the market as well. In this chapter we'll first address why eBay and the Internet have become so popular. Then we'll address how eBay has impacted the other major secondary market selling platforms that have traditionally existed. And finally we will talk about how you can begin selling on eBay (assuming that you are not already doing so).

What Make eBay and the Internet So Popular?

eBay is open 24/7/365. Part of the beauty of eBay and the Internet is that it never closes. *Antique Shows* are typically held only on weekends, usually from 10:00 AM - 5:00 PM. Although held both on weekends and weekdays, *Flea Markets* usually start early in the morning, and close early in the afternoon. *Antique Shops* also have limited hours, with many open only on weekends. This arrangement worked well when there was no competition from any other major selling platform, and when the buying segment had nowhere else to shop for most forms of secondary market *Personal Property*. This all are changed with the advent of the Internet.

Today people can buy or sell on eBay, or anywhere else on the Internet, before they go to work in the morning, or when they return home in the evening. They can shop from their computer at work (so long as their boss doesn't find out). They can shop in the middle of the night. And they can shop in their pajamas or nightgowns if they prefer. This appeals to many people.

Shopping on the Internet is free. There are no admission fees as with Antique Shows. There is also no travel time or expenses required. No hotel fees. No airfare. No gasoline. No tolls.

With gas today costing nearly $3.00-$4.00 per gallon, the money you save by not driving can now be spent on the Internet.

Cheaper Prices and A Worldwide Market. eBay and Internet prices are usually cheaper on more common commodities. Competition forces sellers to lower their price in order to sell more product. If you're looking to buy things like books, MP3 players, CD's, video games, or other type of mass-produced items, you can shop the Internet and look for the best price. When Amazon has 25 sellers offering the same book title, competition forces sellers to lower their price, or risk not selling that item, because buyers like me almost always look for the lowest priced item possible.

In the old days, (i.e. the 1980's) competition for Antiques & Collectibles was pretty much local, or regional at best. The Internet changed that. eBay and the Internet opened up the secondary *Personal Property* markets to a worldwide audience, making things available to anyone anywhere. Whoever thought that you could sell your well-used Levi blue jeans to a European teenager? Today's shoppers can locate items that are being sold anywhere in the world, while sellers can sell to buyers located anywhere throughout the world. The Internet has leveled the playing field. And with the right merchandise the little guys can reach the same markets as the largest Auction Companies in New York and London, or the largest retailers in Hong Kong or Shanghai.

Greater Personal Control. Another major advantage of eBay and the Internet is that it gives sellers greater control over their merchandise. Until the advent of the Internet Auctioneers pretty much controlled the selling process. You consigned your merchandise to them, and the Auctioneers sold it at *Absolute Auction* without limit or reserve. It sold in front of a local audience, or regional audience at best. And it brought what it brought. Sellers had little control over the selling process.

Today's sellers have more options and significantly more control than ever before, thanks to the Internet. For example with an eBay Auction, sellers have the ability to:
*   Tell potential buyers what they feel their item is worth by setting Low & High Estimates of Value.
*   They can set the Starting Price.
*   They can protect themselves by setting a Reserve Price.
*   The can describe the item in any manner they choose.
*   They can promote it with photos of their choosing.
*   They can set the time when the Auction will start and end.
*   They can sell to a national market, and even an international market, if they choose.
*   They can sell without a Buyer's Premium, thereby receiving an even larger return.
*   They can sell with a lower commission, because they are doing all of the work.

Everyone likes more control in their lives, and eBay and the Internet give sellers the ability to control more of their own selling situation.

* * * * * * * * * *

Let's talk about how the Internet has impacted the more traditional secondary market selling platforms that we have already talked about, i.e., Antique Shows, Antique Shops, Flea Markets, and Auctions.

Antique Shows. Antique Shows have probably been hurt more by eBay than any other single selling platform. The mathematics of running Antique Shows are fairly simple. Usually the booth or exhibition fees collected by the Show Promoter cover all of the show expenses, including:

- Facility Rent
- Advertising
- Printing of Show Cards & Posters
- Postage
- Staffing
- Insurance
- Booth Draperies, Walls, etc.

Promoters typically relied upon the Show Gate for their profit. But in today's market, with a declining number of dealers exhibiting at Antique Shows, and with Show Gates declining, promoters are having a significantly more difficult time showing a profit. A large winter show in a major metropolitan area is a perfect example. For nearly 20 years this show had been a premier show boasting 600+ dealers, with dealers exhibiting on two levels within a major convention center. They had an *"Early Buyers"* event on Friday evening from 5:00-9:00 PM, which the dealers hated, but which they were forced to do because the promoter called all of the shots.

But as the Antiques & Collectibles market softened, and as an increasing number of dealers began either leaving the business or reducing the number of shows on their show schedule, the promoters were forced to give up the Friday night *Early Buying* event, and return the show to a two day event, just to accommodate the dealers. Too many dealers were refusing to do a 3-day show. Today this show seems to have less than 50% of the exhibitors they had at the show's peak, and the show today is only on one floor. In effect the show has shrunk in size by nearly 50%.

This is no reflection upon the show itself or its promoters. Rather, it is simply a reflection upon the state of the Antiques & Collectibles business today. We've seen the same thing happening to Antique shows around the country. Major shows are shrinking, smaller shows are dying out, and there are more shows closing than opening.

And much of this is due to the effects of eBay and the Internet.

Antiques Shops. The *Individual Antiques Shop* is all but a relic today. Most have closed their doors because there's not enough traffic to make it profitable.

The same can be said for *Group Shops*. In the 1980's most Group Shops were strong. Better shops carried great merchandise, selected only the best dealers to exhibit in their shops, and held their dealers to high standards of merchandise. Better shops turned away more potential exhibiting dealers than they allowed in.

Today with the number of Antiques Dealers decreasing, most Group Shops are having a very difficult time filling their shops with quality dealers. In order to cover the rent, shop owners have been forced to either accept lower-end merchandise, or reproductions or crafts. This may have helped them along for a few additional months, but eventually the customer traffic flow begins to decline, which led to a decline in dealer sales, which led more dealers to quit those specific shops, thereby forcing many Group Shops to close their doors. As with Antique Shows, there are more Antiques Shops closing than opening today.

Flea Markets. Flea Markets have also shown a serious decline from the 1980's. My long-time favorite Flea Market is located in Lambertville NJ. Actually it was two Flea Markets located side-by-side which attracted exhibitors from beyond a 3-state area. Lambertville had a lower level, and an upper level. In the 1980s, both levels were almost always filled to capacity. You needed to call well in advance in order to reserve a booth, or you took your chances of missing a selling day on any given weekend. Today I can't recall the last time this market was operating at full capacity.

The reason Flea Markets, Antique Shops, and Antique Shows are all having a difficult time surviving today is because there are fewer dealers. And there are fewer dealers because many are leaving the business because of a drop in sales, or they have opted to move to eBay or some other Internet selling venue, where they can sell at lower expense, without having to pack and unpack their merchandise, without having to get up at 3:00-4:00 AM, and, without having to endure the extreme and inclement weather outdoors.

Auctions. Auctions have probably been impacted less by eBay and the Internet than the other traditional selling platforms, but Auctions have indeed felt its impact. One of the reasons that Auctions have been less impacted by eBay is that eBay sellers need a source of fresh merchandise to sell on the Internet. Auctions offer that source because Auctions are where fresh merchandise comes to market, through either the sale of estates, downsized homes, excess dealer inventory, or cleanouts.

Traditionally there has been an unwritten bond between Auctioneers and Antiques Dealers. By that I mean dealers need Auctioneers in order to acquire fresh merchandise in the most economical manner possible. But on the other hand Auctioneers need dealers to buy their merchandise. In an ideal world it would be nice to think that Auctioneers could always sell their consignments at the retail level. But that is simply impossible. Auctioneers handle too much merchandise to sell it all at retail prices levels. They need dealers to buy the remaining items that fail to sell at the retail level. So the truth is that Auctioneers need dealers as much as dealers need the Auctioneers.

But all is not rosy for the Auction business either. Because dealers are selling less, they are buying less. And with an increasing number of dealers dropping out of the business, there are fewer potential buyers at Auction from the 1990's market peak level. Auctioneers work on a commission basis, which means that if gross sales are dropping due to declining prices, revenues are dropping as well. Yet Auction expenses are not dropping. Which means that the profitability of many Auctioneers has been decreasing as well.

All due to the effects of the Internet.

I'll Bet Most of Your Have Never Heard of Sniping Software

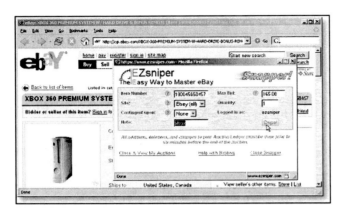

When I spoke at the 2007 *Pennsylvania Auctioneers Convention*, I asked the Auctioneers in attendance how many had ever *"Sniped"* an eBay Auction. Not one Auctioneer raised their hand.

I then asked the Auctioneers how many owned *"Sniping Software"*. Again, no one raised their hand.

I then asked the group how many even knew what *"Sniping Software"* even was. And again, no one raised their hand. This was a group of some of the top Auctioneers in the country, and no one had any idea what *"Auction Sniping Software"* was.

So, what is *"Auction Sniping Software"*? Sniping Software is an inexpensive and easy-to-use and install software that Internet Auction buyers can add to their computer which enables their computer to bid for them on eBay Auctions without even having to be at their computer.

Have you ever watched an eBay Auction closely? All too often there will be few, if any, bids during the entire 7-day duration of the Auction. But then, in the last 30 seconds of the Auction, 10-20 bids come in at around the same time. Did you think that all of those people were sitting at their computer, waiting for the Auction to end, and then all keying in their final bids within seconds of the Auction's end? Maybe that's the way it used to be in the early days of eBay, but it's not the way it is today. Rather, most of those last minute bids were being placed by Auction Sniping Software. These bidders placed their bids hours or days prior to the end of the Auction, and then simply let their computer do the rest, while the actual bidders are off doing something else. Sniping Software has changed the way Internet bidders can bid. Bidders no longer have to sit at their computer waiting for an Auction to end. They simply punch a few keys, and let their Sniping Software to the rest for them. They can go shopping, play tennis, handle yard work, whatever they want to do. And their computer will handle all of their eBay bidding for them.

There are many different types of sniping software. I use a program called *AuctionSentry.com*. This *Auction Sniping Software* can be purchased on eBay for as little as $14.95. If you're interested in sniping any eBay Auctions, you can purchase your Sniping Software today, pay for it with PayPal, immediately download it, and have it working within only a matter of minutes.

There are actually only three basic steps to using Auction Sniping Software.

1) *Cut and Paste the eBay Auction Number*. Each eBay Auction item has a unique 11-12 digit descriptive code. Once you locate the item that you want to bid on, highlight that 11-12 digit eBay code, copy it, and paste into the appropriate box on the Sniping Software screen.

2) *Place Your Maximum Bid*. In another field you place your maximum bid. This is not your starting but, but rather the maximum amount that your Sniping Software will bid for you. It doesn't start at that amount, but rather bids for you in the standard bid increments as defined by eBay, until it reaches your maximum bid. As a result you can often win an Auction at an amount far below your maximum bid.

3) *Set Your Preferred Snipe Time*. I use 9 seconds. Some people prefer only 1 or 2 seconds. But this is the beauty of Sniping Software.

The Auction Sniping Software does the rest. I am not trying to convince you to acquire Sniping Software, especially during your *Home Downsizing* phase. Rather my point here is that wouldn't you rather have as many people as possible bidding on your merchandise? Sniping software is just another tool that makes it easier for buyers to spend money on the Internet.

Sell It Yourself On eBay

As we've discussed, eBay has become increasingly popular with many sellers over the past ten years. It may or may not be for you. eBay allows sellers to easily do business on the Internet, with little of the time or expense it takes to open a bricks and motor store. Hours are flexible, the expense is reasonable, you work want when you want to, and you don't work when you don't want to work. The Internet gives you the broadest possible audience for whatever it is that you're selling. For many sellers, eBay has provided an entirely new livelihood.

But there are many disadvantages to selling on eBay as well. Probably the biggest disadvantage is the time and effort that is required to sell on eBay. In our experience we have seen that it takes approximately one hour per item to sell on eBay. This will vary by what you are selling, but selling on eBay takes time because there are ten tasks that have to be completed in order to wrap up each eBay sale.

1. *Describe It*. The first thing you must do is describe what you are selling in order to make a potential buyer want to purchase something that they have never seen or held in person. You must describe it in detail, and include High & Low Estimates, a Starting Price, and a Reserve, if you choose to sell with a Reserve. You will also have to specify your shipping costs, delivery terms, and terms & conditions of sale. Perhaps the most important part of the description is "*Condition*", which must be described in detail. If you fail to describe any flaws, in all likelihood the merchandise will be returned.

2. *Photograph It*. Clear and crisp color digital images are a must. Photograph the front, back, sides, top & bottoms of the items if appropriate. Photograph any markings, signatures, names etc. that will help to convince the potential buyer that it is authentic. Photograph any damage. If you try the hide the damage in your description, you will get the item back, and receive negative feedback. This is almost guaranteed. Remember to use the VGA image size or lowest setting possible. Higher resolution images, which are better for printing, take forever to open on the Internet. If a potential buyer cannot get your pictures to open, they will look for something else to buy.

3. *Edit the Images*. It is usually best if you edit the images in order to make them show better on the Internet. Almost any image editing software program will enable you to crop, rotate, brighten, and/or sharpen your digital images to make them appear clearer.

4. *List It*. Next you want to upload your description and images to eBay and start the Auction. If selling only a few items, eBay's standard listing tools will suffice. If listing more than a few, you perhaps may want to download eBay's *"Turbo Lister"* free listing tool. But if you plan on getting serious about listing items on eBay, you will probably want to use one of the commercially available eBay Listing tools available on the Internet. They offer many tools which will simplify and speed-up the listing process if you are listing a large number of items.

5. *Answer questions promptly*. You will invariably receive questions about what you are selling. Usually the questions are about condition or shipping expense. If you fail to answer these questions, you will lose that potential buyer of your merchandise.

6. *Send an Invoice*. Once the sale is completed, send the winning bidder an invoice. eBay makes this easy for you to do. The faster you send the invoice, the faster you will get paid.

7. *Collect Payment and Handle the Banking*. Most likely you will use PayPal. Most eBay buyers and sellers do. It's safe, convenient, and sometimes enables you to be paid almost immediately after the Auction is over.

8. *Package It*. For many, this is the worst part of the eBay process. You must find a box, and wrap and package the sold item so that it will promptly and safely arrive at its final destination. For most items, finding the right box will be easy. For some items, finding the right box may take days. Think about how you will be shipping something *before* you list it on eBay.

9. *Ship It*. Once you have been paid, and after you have packaged the item, you need to ship it. Most packages are shipped through the Post Office, UPS, or one of the other major delivery carriers. Occasionally a winning bidder will want to pick up the item from you personally in order to save on the shipping expense.

10. *Leave Feedback*. Feedback is the backbone of the eBay system. Leave it for your buyers and they will leave it for you.

What Does It Cost To Sell On eBay?

If you sell via Public Auction, the Auctioneer will normally charge you a commission that represents a flat percentage of the final selling price. Rarely are there other charges. (We'll discuss more on this in Chapter 17).

eBay, on the other hand, has a fee-structure that is complicated, and although the individual fees may not seem all that expensive, by the time you add them up they can sometimes be comparable to what you will pay at Public Auction, except that you are doing all of the work.

Basically there are three types of fees involved with selling on eBay:
- Insertion Fees
- Final Value Fees
- Listing Upgrade Fees

Insertion Fees: This is the fee that eBay charges you simply to list an item on eBay. You will pay this fee whether your items sell or not. Listing fees will vary from as low a $.10-$.15 per item, up to $4.00 per item. (All fees listed here were current as this book was written. eBay raises its fees regularly and these fees may or may not be totally accurate as you are reading this book). The lower the starting or reserve price, the lower the Insertion Fee. eBay encourages lower starting or reserve prices with lower Insertion Fees primarily because eBay will not collect its final Value Fees unless an item sells. Lower starting or reserve prices mean that more items will sell.

Final Value Fee: This is the fee that eBay charges you once an item sells. This fee is only payable once an item sells, and it will vary based upon the final selling price.

- $01 - $25.00   8.75% of the closing value

- $25.01 - $1,000.00   8.75% of the initial $25.00 ($2.19)
                        Plus 3.5% of the remaining closing value

- $1,000.01+   8.75% of the initial $25.00 ($2.19)
                        Plus 3.5% of the next $25.01-$1,000.00 (up to $34.12 at this level)
                        Plus 1.5% of the remaining closing value

Listing Upgrade Fees: This is where things can really add up if you are not careful. The cost of these *Listing Upgrade Fees* can vary between $.10 - $79.95+. Examples of Listing Upgrade Fees include:
- Value Pack
- Gallery Plus
- Listing Designer
- Subtitle
- Boldface
- Scheduled Listing
- 10-Day Auction Duration
- Gift Services
- Border
- Highlight
- Gallery Featured

91

- Home Page Featured (Single Item)
- Home Page Featured (Multiple Items)
- Listing in 2 Categories

You Can't Sell on eBay If You Don't Use PayPal

For all practical purposes, you can't sell on eBay if you don't use PayPal. PayPal is an on-line payment service, similar to a credit card, which allows users to transfer funds electronically. Whereas wire transfers were the quickest and easiest way to transfer money during the 20th century, PayPal has become the preferred method of on-line payment early in the 21st century. Using special encryption software, PayPal allows users to make financial transfers between computers at the click of a button, which has stimulated the growth of Internet commerce. Today PayPal boasts more than 100,000,000 accounts worldwide.

Anyone can sign up for a free PayPal account and the concept is quite simple. Rather than providing an account # (bank account, credit card, debit card, etc.) to each individual or business you deal with on-line, you apply for a PayPal account and give PayPal a single account number. Then each time you authorize PayPal to make a payment for you, the recipient only receives your payment, but no sensitive account information, which helps to protect your privacy and identity.

You can send funds to anyone with an e-mail address, even if they don't have a PayPal account. However, in order to retrieve their funds, they will also have to apply for a PayPal account, and any funds transferred via PayPal will remain in a PayPal account until the funds are retrieved.

It costs you nothing to make a payment using PayPal. However a small fee, similar to a Visa or MasterCard processing fee, will be charged against the recipient of the money, just as a merchant who accepts a credit card payment is charged. And in exchange for this small charge, the seller has almost instantaneous access to their money, which is generally far better that waiting many days for a check to arrive.

PayPal is a relatively new concept and was only founded in 1998. It was acquired by eBay in 2002 and has added considerably to eBay's growth. At the time this book was going to press, eBay had just announced that PayPal would become, for all practical purposes, the only payment medium allowed with eBay transactions. So, if you want to sell on eBay, you must use PayPal. For further details, visit: www.PayPal.com

* * * * * * * * *

What Equipment Is Needed To Sell on the Internet?

If you don't have the right equipment, or if you do not understand computers or the Internet, you will not be able to list items on eBay by yourself. At the minimum you will need the following:

- Computer, with a current operating system and an adequate amount of RAM
- Digital Camera

- Image Editing Software
- eBay Listing Software
- Internet Access
- E-Mail
- PayPal

eBay Advantages
- The Internet offers a huge base of national and international buyers.
- The expense can be reasonable, although fees are continually rising.
- It's fun for some.
- You can work at home.
- You can dispose of items you no longer want or need.
- It gives you the opportunity to receive top dollar.

eBay Disadvantages
- If you don't have the tools, computer or Internet knowledge, or someone to help you with this, selling on eBay is not for you.
- The time involved in selling items on eBay can sometimes come to one hour or more per item.
- There are a wide variety of expenses
  - eBay Insertion Fees
  - eBay Final Value Fees
  - Listing Upgrade Fees
  - PayPal or Credit Card Expense
  - Packing Materials
  - Shipping Expense
- What do you do with the items that fail to sell on eBay?

eBay Summary: For many, selling on eBay may be one of the best options for disposing of certain merchandise for Fair Market Value. But for others the time commitment, amount of work involved, and other concerns may lead certain sellers to one of the other available selling options. And since everything you own will not sell on eBay, you should consider a eBay as only one of several selling options, not the only option available to you.

Home Downsizing Tips

✓ eBay and the Internet have changed the way that Antiques, Collectibles, and Household Items are sold.

✓ Part of the beauty of the Internet is that it never closes. It's open 24/7/365.

✓ eBay offers Sellers almost total control over the selling process by allowing the Seller to define all important aspects of the sale.

✓ When photographing items for the Internet, always be certain to use the *"VGA"* format. Larger-sized images will take longer to open and will reduce your overall sales.

✓ Auction Sniping Software allows bids to bid from their computers when they are not even there.

✓ For many eBay is the perfect selling platform because of the flexibility it offers in so many different areas.

✓ Although eBay is the preferred selling platform for many, the time commitment that is required to sell on eBay (est. 1 hour per item) deters many people who don't have the time or patience to handle such a business.

✓ The two most important keys to selling on eBay or the Internet are clear and detailed photographs, and a clear statement of condition. If you fail to describe any condition issues associated with your item, you will get it back and you will receive negative feedback from the disgruntled buyer.

---

eBay Listing Services: If we locate any treasures deserving of national and international exposure during our *In-Home Personal Property Walk-Through Valuation*, we can list if for you on eBay. We are *eBay* and *eBay Live Auction PowerSellers* as well as certified *eBay Trading Assistants* and have nearly 10 years of *eBay* selling experience. We can handle your *eBay* listing chores in a prompt and professional manner and help you to convert your newly-found treasures into cash. Contact us for further details.

Chapter 14

Selling It Through eBay Drop Shops

Auctioneers hate them. So do Antique Dealers. Over the past several years *eBay Drop Shops* have become one of the fastest growing businesses in America. Sometimes called *eBay Drop-Off Stores or Centers*, today there are nearly 10,000 of them across the country, with new ones opening up every day.

What is an *eBay Drop Shop*? An *eBay Drop Shop* is a store where you can take your merchandise to have it listed on eBay. Without having to do any work, you can take your merchandise to an *eBay Drop Shop* and they will list it on eBay for you...in exchange for a fee.

Many individuals prefer listing their own Auction items on eBay. They like writing the descriptions, taking and editing the digital images, setting the minimum prices and reserves, and managing their own on-line Auctions. By doing it themselves they save a considerable amount of money.

Other people, however, prefer to have someone else do it for them. Either they don't have computer savvy, they don't understand the eBay listing process, or they simply don't have time to do it. Their lives are too busy and they just don't want to do it themselves. Enter the *eBay Drop Shop*.

Many *eBay Drop Shops* are individual shops, owned by a single individual or family. Working out of their home or local storefront, these are primarily local businesses. Some are full-time businesses, others are part-time.

Other *eBay Drop Shops* are part of a larger national chain or franchise, participating in a huge network of national stores. *usaAuctionDrop*, *i-SoldIt*, and *e-PowerSellers* are just three of a rapidly growing number of *eBay Drop Shop* franchises that are popping up around the country. But whether individual business or franchise, the key thing that these shops offer is their knowledge of the eBay process, and their ability to turn your excess merchandise into cash.

AuctionDrop has signed a deal with UPS to offer walk-in Auction consignment services in conjunction with nearly 3,700 UPS Stores around the country, thereby making it the country's largest eBay Drop Off franchise.

eBay Drop Shops have been growing so quickly over the past five years that some of the smaller, less well-run businesses, have been closing their doors as the competition heats up. But although the growth of the *eBay Drop Shops* may be slowing down a little, there is no doubt that the *eBay Drop Shop* is here to stay.

95

How Does The Process Work? It's actually quite simple. You take your merchandise to the eBay store, and they will do all of the work. You must usually sign a contract which lists the Terms & Conditions under which they will sell your merchandise, and it will (should) explain the costs and fees involved. The eBay Drop Shop then lists your items on eBay, collects the money, and deducts the eBay fees, their commissions and other approved expenses, and sends you the remainder as payment for your merchandise.

But the fees are where things can get fairly complicated. Most eBay Shops have different fee structures, so it often becomes difficult to compare the bottom line cost between shops. However, generally they include the following:

- *The eBay Drop Shop's Commission*. We have seen these commissions varying between 15%-40+%
  - Some eBay Drop Shops charge a flat commission, based upon the final selling price. (e.g., 35% of the final selling price)
  - Others charge a sliding commission scale, with a decreasing commission on various selling price levels (e.g., 40% on the first $200, 30% on the next $300, etc.)
- *All eBay Listing Fees, Final Value Fees, and Listing Upgrade Fees*: See Chapter 13 for how these fees work.

So although you may not be doing any of the work, you will be paying for someone else to do it, often in the range of 50% of the final selling price after all commissions and fees are deducted from your final check. To some, 50% may seem like an outrageous amount. To others, 50% of something is better than 100% of nothing. You will have to decide whether the *eBay Drop Shop* is the right option for you.

Can eBay Drop Shops Sell Everything on eBay? Unfortunately no. Certain things will sell very well on eBay, such as:

- Most forms of Antiques & Collectibles
- Named merchandise
- Smaller and easily-shippable items
- Items in clean and unblemished condition

However, other items are very difficult to sell on eBay.

- Larger items (most common furniture)
- Un-named merchandise (knick-knacks, chochkees, etc.)
- Items in less than perfect condition.

It's tough to go into much more detail about what sells and what does not sell well on eBay here, but the eBay Drop Shop should know whether your items will sell or not.

What If Your Items Fail To Sell. Most *eBay Drop Shops* won't accept merchandise that they don't think they can sell, so that should minimize the problem. In the event that something doesn't sell, you will typically be responsible for picking it up, paying for the return shipping, or having the store dispose of it, which can possibly lead to you having to pay a hefty disposal fee. Be sure to read your paperwork carefully on this before consigning.

Are There Alternatives to eBay Drop Shops?

eBay Trading Assistants: eBay sponsors what they call their *Trading Assistant Program*. *Trading Assistants* are not eBay employees or independent contractors of eBay. Nor does eBay endorse or approve them. Rather, *Trading Assistants* run their own independent business, without any involvement from eBay.

To become an eBay *Trading Assistant* and to be listed in the *eBay Trading Assistant Directory*, candidates must agree to and abide by the *eBay Trading Assistant User Agreement*, and they must reside in the United States.

In addition, *Trading Assistants* must:
- Have an eBay account in good standing at all times.
- Have sold at least ten (10) items on eBay in the previous three (3) months and maintain 10 sales per 3-month period.
- Maintain a minimum feedback rating of 100, with at least 98% positive feedback rating at all times.
- Abide by the terms of the *Trading Assistant Style Guide*.

To locate an eBay *Trading Assistant* near you, you can go to eBay's Web Site (www.ebay.com) and key in your Zip Code and eBay will provide you with a listing of the *Trading Assistants* closest to you.

As you can see, these are not very stringent guidelines, and you should apply the same standards in selecting a *Trading Assistant* as you would in hiring an *eBay Drop Shop*.

eBay Drop Shop Advantages
- They offer you the ability to access a large base of potential national & international buyers if you are unable to do it yourself.
- Someone else does all of your work.
- They offer you the ability to achieve higher prices than if you were only selling locally.
- They allow you to dispose of items you no longer want or need.
- For some, the expense will seem reasonable.

eBay Drop Shop Disadvantages
- For others, the expense may seem unreasonable.
- Not everything can be sold on eBay.
- What to do with unsold items?

Home Downsizing Tips

✓ Select an *eBay Drop Shop* that has considerable eBay listing experience and which has an excellent reputation. Check the *eBay Drop Shop's* eBay Feedback to help determine their reputation.

✓ Closely inspect the costs involved with selling at any given *eBay Drop Shop.*

✓ Get the Terms & Conditions of selling through any *eBay Drop Shop,* as well as their commission and fee schedule, before you give them any merchandise.

✓ Get everything in writing before you deliver any merchandise.

---

eBay Listing Services: If we locate any treasures deserving of national and international exposure during our *In-Home Personal Property Walk-Through Valuation,* we can list if for you on eBay. We are *eBay* and *eBay Live Auction PowerSellers* as well as certified *eBay Trading Assistants* and have nearly 10 years of *eBay* selling experience. We can handle your *eBay* listing chores in a prompt and professional manner and help you to convert your newly-found treasures into cash. Contact us for further details.

Chapter 15

Sell It Privately...If You Can Find the Right Buyer

For many the thought of selling their excess *Personal Property* privately offers the best of all worlds. They can receive a known amount of money, without any commissions, without any time delay, and without any uncertainty. There are no strangers coming into their house, and they can sell with the least amount of difficulty.

In the old days (i.e., prior to the 1980's), this was relatively easy. In a small local community, you simply called the Auctioneer, Antiques Dealer, or the Junkman, worked out a deal, and they took all. No hassles. No delays.

Today things have gotten more difficult. There are so many options available to sellers, they often times don't know which way to turn. Who do you trust?

Who should you sell to privately?

- *Friends & Neighbors*: Friends and neighbors often represent the easiest form of private sale. Your friends and neighbors know what you have, and they know that you're downsizing. And often they may have an interest in the items that you are selling. So try them first. The biggest question when dealing with family and friends is...*What is the fairest price to charge*? You don't want to ask too much because they are your friends, but you don't want to give it away either. What is the fairest price? You will have to decide what is fair to both of you.

- *Antique Dealers*: If you have a quantity of better Antiques or Collectibles, you may want to invite in the Antiques dealer. Antiques dealers specialize in buying and selling Antiques and Collectibles. They understand the value of these things, they understand what is and is not selling in the local market, and they understand how to sell them. If you know an honest and reputable Antiques dealer, you can often invite them in to make you a fair market offer on what you are selling. Sometimes this represents the easiest way to dispose of your Personal Property, assuming that the dealer you're working with will make you a fair market offer.

- *Non-Antique Consignment Shops*: If you have a quantity of better household merchandise, items that aren't really Antiques or Collectibles, but are still nice,

99

clean, and very usable household items, you might consider bringing in a representative from the local Consignment Shop. Unlike Antique Consignment Shops which deal only in Antiques, General Consignment Shops deal with household items more than Antiques. They don't want to deal in things that are highly used, damaged, blemished, or technologically out of date. They are often interested in purchasing items such as microwave ovens, clothing, silver plate serving pieces, good-quality China, and other such items that may not be Antiques, but are still certainly desirable and usable in today's typical household. They understand that the best way to re-sell used household merchandise is to offer it at a low price, so don't expect them to offer you top dollar on your used items. But sometimes this option can resolve your situation quickly and easily.

- *Cleanout Specialist*: Sometimes called the *"Junkman"*, today's *Cleanout Specialists* can offer more than just taking out the junk. In Chapter 22 we'll introduce you to the *Cleanout Specialist*, but at this point you simply need to understand that there are people whom you can call to clean out your house of any and all items that you simply don't want anymore. They may purchase it outright, or they may charge you to take it away, but in certain circumstances they may offer the best alternative.

- *Auctioneers*: In some areas you may want to consider bringing in the local Auctioneer. There are some Auctioneers who simply do not buy households, estates, antiques or collectibles, or excess *Personal Property* because they feel that this could represent a conflict of interest. These Auctioneers are always seeking to accept quality consignments to Auction, but they do not buy outright. Other Auctioneers are always willing to buy outright. They do not perceive this to be a conflict of interest, and sometimes they may represent the best single source to purchase it all, including your better Antiques & Collectibles, household items, and even your junk. The primary advantage of selling to Auctioneers is that the Auctioneer understands pricing, knows what they can sell the merchandise for, so therefore they know what they have to pay in order to make a fair profit. We'll talk more about Auctioneers and the entire Auction-selling process in Chapter 17. But at this point, you simply need to understand that in certain circumstances the Auctioneer may represent a good source to take all of your excess personal property.

What is the best approach to privately selling your excess *Personal Property*? We would recommend the following steps to help you successfully sell your merchandise privately:

- *First Understand Value*: Before doing anything, develop an understanding of the general value of what you are selling…*before offering it for sale*. Otherwise, how do you know if you are receiving a fair offer? We have already discussed how you can do this. But whether you do the research yourself, or bring in an outside appraiser, you *must* understand what something may be worth before selling it.

- *Seek Out Specialists*: Don't sell to the first buyer who comes along. Seek out qualified potential buyers. By *"qualified"* buyers, we mean buyers who understand what you are selling. Don't offer your china to a baseball card dealer; don't offer your coins and stamps to a furniture dealer.

- *Get Multiple Offers*: Always get at least three firm offers from qualified potential buyers. If selling coins and stamps, don't sell to the first coin & stamp dealer that you speak to. Get three offers from three coin & stamp dealers. You may be surprised at the variance in the three offers.

- *Be Clear On What You Are Selling*. A potential buyer cannot make you a fair and firm offer unless they know exactly what they are buying. Leave no room for misunderstanding.

- *It's OK to Negotiate*: Be prepared to negotiate on price. If you state a price, the potential buyer will almost always offer you less. If the potential buyer offers you a price, you can and should ask for more. Plan to meet somewhere in to middle so both of you leave happy. Negotiating is part of the process.

- *Which Offer Do You Accept?:* After analyzing your offers, accept what you feel is the fairest offer. Sometimes price will be the key factor. Other times *whom* you are selling it to, or *where* it is going, will mean more to you than the money.

- *Leave Room for the Buyer to Make a Profit*: Recognize that almost any potential buyer will need to make a fair profit. They will be tying up their money, they will have expenses, they will be doing the work, and they are entitled to make a fair profit. Leave room in your pricing accordingly.

- *Ask for Cash*: Don't be afraid to ask for cash payment. Checks can bounce, and sometimes cash-in-hand just feels better than a paper check.

- *Contact the Under-bidders*: After the deal has been completed, give the under-bidders (those whose offers you did not accept) the courtesy of a call, letting them know that you have disposed of your item(s) elsewhere, and thanking them for their offer.

The biggest disadvantage of selling privately is not knowing whether you received a fair offer or not. If you have done your homework, this should not be a problem. If you know who you are dealing with, and if they are reputable, this should not be a problem. Just be certain of what you are selling...*before you let it go.*

* * * * * * * *

Advantages of Private Sale
- You can make a quick sale with little or no work.
- You will receive a known amount.
- The buyer will haul it away at their expense.
- No commissions or moving expenses will have to be paid.
- Cash payment is a possibility and can be requested as part of the deal.

Disadvantages of Private Sale
- Who do you sell to?
- Lingering questions, such as:
  - Did you truly receive Fair Market Value?
  - Did you sell too quickly?
  - Was there a better buyer out there somewhere?
- If you haven't done your homework, you may never know.

Home Downsizing Tips

✓ Understand the value of what you are selling before, not after, you sell it privately (or any other way).

✓ Don't sell it all to the first person who comes along. If selling privately, get at least three offers from different potential buyers. You will probably be surprised at the variance in offer prices.

✓ Rarely will someone want it buy it all at the best possible price. Sometimes the best thing to do is sell it privately by commodity. For example, sell the furniture to a Furniture Dealer, the Art to an Art Dealer, the China & Glass to a Glass Dealer, etc.

✓ We all want to sell everything we own for top dollar. Rarely will this occur. In order to sell everything within a reasonable amount of time, you must leave some room in your selling price for the buyer to also make a reasonable profit.

✓ Visit www.collectors.org or www.collectoronline.com in order to find the largest grouping of Collectors Clubs to be found anywhere on the Internet.

Chapter 16

Donate It to the Cause of Your Choice

For many people, an important part of the *Home Downsizing* process involves making a charitable contribution of some of their *Personal Property*. Sometimes it involves donating an important piece of art or furniture to a local museum. Other times it involves making a cash gift to a favorite institution or cause. For those who are simply interested in donating *Personal Property* out of the goodness of their heart, without taking a tax deduction, the process is relatively easy. But if you intend to take a tax write-off for your donation, things get much more complicated.

The objective of this chapter is to discuss the general guidelines for donating money or *Personal Property* gifts. This chapter is not intended to provide legal, accounting, or financial advice. You should consult your legal or financial counsel for this. Rather the intention of this chapter is to give you a very general overview of what may be involved if you wish to donate some of your *Personal Property* during your *Home Downsizing*.

The primary IRS document regarding charitable donations is *IRS Publication 526: Charitable Contributions*. This document can be found at, and printed out in its 23-page PDF format at: www.irs.gov

This publication is quite precise (hence, complicated), as is pretty much any IRS form. But in this chapter we will try to bring out some of the general guidelines that may be involved in donating any of your excess *Personal Property*. But once again be sure to consult with your legal and financial counsel before doing anything in this area.

We'll start with one very simple point: *In order to deduct charitable donations from your taxes, you need to itemize your deductions.* If you do not itemize your deductions, but instead take the standard deduction, you will receive no tax benefit from your charitable donation.

A second important point is that in order for any charitable donation to be considered tax deductable, it must be made to a *"qualified"* organization. *IRS Publication 526* defines a charitable contribution as follows: *A charitable contribution is a donation or gift to, or for the use of, a qualified organization. It is voluntary and is made without getting, or expecting to get, anything of equal value.*

An important part of this definition is *"a qualified organization"*. Contributions are only deductible if made to a qualified organization. Other than churches and governments (which automatically qualify), groups must apply to the IRS in order to become *"qualified"*. Once approved by the IRS as a qualified organization, this group will be listed in *IRS Publication 78*.

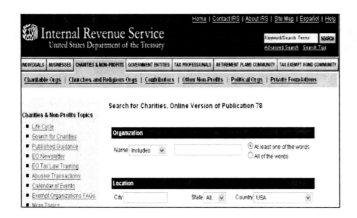

There are several ways to determine whether a group you are considering donating to is *"qualified"*. First, you can ask the group if they are qualified, and most will know whether they are or not. However, to be 100% certain, you can visit *IRS Publication 78* online and make a determination whether that group is actually on the government's list of qualified organizations at this web address: http://www.irs.gov/app/pub-78/

In very general terms, according to *IRS Publication 526*, money or *Personal Property* you gave to the following groups <u>*are deductible*</u> as Charitable Contributions
- Churches, Synagogues, Temples, Mosques, and other Religious Organizations.
- Federal, State, and Local Governments, if your contribution is solely for public purposes (e.g., a gift to reduce the public debt).
- Nonprofit Schools and Hospitals.
- Public Parks and Recreation Facilities.
- Salvation Army, Red Cross, CARE, Goodwill Industries, United Way, Boy Scouts, Girl Scouts, Boys and Girls Clubs of America, etc.
- War Veterans' Groups.
- Charitable organizations listed in *Publication 78*.

Also according to *IRS Publication 526*, money or *Personal Property* you give to the following <u>*are not deductible*</u> as Charitable Contributions
- Specific Individuals.
- A Contribution to a Non-Qualified Organization.
- Civic Leagues, Social and Sports Clubs, Labor Unions, and Chambers of Commerce.
- Foreign Organizations (except certain Canadian, Israeli, and Mexican charities).
- Groups that are run for personal profit.
- Groups whose purpose is to lobby for law changes.
- Homeowners' Associations.
- Political Groups or Candidates for Public Office.
- The part of a contribution from which you receive or expect to receive a benefit.
- The value of your time or service.
- Your personal expenses.
- Appraisal fees.

<u>*What Can You Donate*</u>? The easiest thing to donate is cash, because its value is so exact.

Generally you can deduct the actual cash amount of what you donate (subject, of course, to certain limitations).

You can also donate non-cash *Personal Property* to qualified organizations, including Art, Antiques, Furniture, Collectibles, Cars, Land, or many other forms of Personal Property. Here, however, you can deduct only the *"Fair Market Value"* of the Personal Property. We briefly touched upon *"Fair Market Value"* in Chapter 6 in our discussion of value. But a significantly more complete definition of the IRS's definition of Personal Property can be found in *IRS Publication 561: Determining the Value of Donated Property".*

However, note that special rules apply if you contribute:

- Clothing or Household Items.
- A Car, Boat, or Airplane.
- Taxidermy Property.
- Property Subject to a Debt.
- A Partial Interest in Property.
- A Fractional Interest in Tangible Personal Property.
- A Qualified Conservation Contribution.
- A Future Interest in Tangible Personal Property.
- Inventory from Your Business.
- A Patent or Other Intellectual Property.

You cannot take a deduction for clothing or household items you donate unless the clothing or household items are in good used condition or better, and with household items being defined as follows:

- Furniture
- Furnishings
- Electronics
- Appliances
- Linens
- Other similar items.

Household items do not include:

- Food
- Paintings, Antiques, and other objects of Art
- Jewelry and Gems
- Collections

<u>*How Much Can You Deduct*</u>? Generally, you can deduct your contributions of money or *Personal Property* that you make to, or for the use of, a qualified organization. A gift or contribution is *"for the use of"* a qualified

105

organization when it is held in a legally enforceable trust for the qualified organization or in a similar legal arrangement.

The contributions must be made to a qualified organization and not set aside for use by a specific person.

If you give property to a qualified organization, you generally can deduct the fair market value of the property at the time of the contribution.

Your deduction for charitable contributions is generally limited to 50% of your adjusted gross income, but in some cases 20% and 30% limits may apply. In addition, the total of your charitable contribution deduction and certain other itemized deductions may be limited. Consult your legal or financial advisors for more specific information in this area.

When Can You Deduct It? You can generally take the tax deduction in the year that the charitable donation was made, but of course there are certain exceptions. Whether you use a cash or accrual method of accounting can make a difference, as well as the form of contribution (cash, check, promissory note, stock certificate, etc). But a good rule of thumb is that the time of its unconditional delivery will serve as the date of donation.

What Records Are Required to Substantiate the Tax Deduction? The kind of records you must keep depend upon the amount of the contribution, and whether it is a cash or non-cash donation.

Cash contributions will vary, depending whether the cash contribution is less than $250, or greater than $250. In most instances you cannot deduct the cash contribution unless you keep one of the following:

- Appropriate bank records.
- A letter or receipt from the qualified organization providing the basic minimum required documentation and date verification.
- Appropriate payroll deduction records.

Non-cash contribution record requirements will vary, depending upon the amount of the deduction.

- *Deductions of less than $250*
    o Need a receipt from the qualified organization showing the basic required information.
    o Additional reliable written records for each item donated.
- *Deductions of at least $250 but not more than $500*
    o Same as above, plus
    o Additional reliable written records including a description of the donated property and a good faith estimate of value.
- *Deductions over $500 but not more than $5,000*
    o Same as above, plus
    o How you got the property.
    o When you received the property.
    o The cost or other basis of the property.
- *Deductions over $5,000*

o   Same as above, plus
o   A qualified written appraisal of the donated property from a qualified appraiser.
o   See Deductions of More Than $5,000 in IRS Publication 561 for additional information.

Donation Advantages

- Donating something of value can provide you with a good feeling.
- You can help a good cause.
- You may receive a possible financial benefit with a tax deduction.
- You can dispose of better items you no longer want or need.

Donation Disadvantages

- The complexity of the tax and legal implications.
- The Appraisal expense.
- The Accountant expense.
- The Legal expense.
- IRS Considerations: What if the IRS voids the transaction?

In Summary: Donating certain important pieces of *Personal Property* may appeal to you. For some, the joy of giving and the feeling of knowing that something very important to you may soon be hanging in a museum or helping your favorite organization may far outweigh the expense and detail required to justify the tax deduction of your charitable contribution.

Home Downsizing Tips

✓   You must itemize your deductions on your tax return in order to receive any tax benefit from your charitable donation.

✓   Your gift must be made to a *"qualified"* organization in order to receive any tax benefit from your charitable donation.

✓   A written appraisal from a qualified appraiser is required on all donated *Personal Property* having a deduction of over $5,000.

✓   The three most important IRS Publications covering Charitable Donations are 78, 526, and 561.

✓   The amount of documentation and record keeping required will vary depending upon the amount of the *"deduction"* amount.

Chapter 17

The Insider's Guide to Selling at Auction

As I said in the third sentence in this book, "*I'm an Auctioneer*". I believe in the *Auction Method of Selling*. I love the Auction profession.

And now, you're probably thinking that as an Auctioneer, I'm going to try to steer you to selling at Auction. Nothing could be further from the truth. While selling at Auction does work for many people and in many situations, there are just as many situations where selling at Auction is not the correct approach. I tell clients that almost every day.

So with that said and done, let's begin this chapter on the possibility of selling your excess *Personal Property* at Auction. I could write an entire book on the Auction business (which is something that I am currently working on). But for purposes of this *Home Downsizing* book, I'll devote this chapter primarily to "*Selling at Auction*", touching only very lightly on "*Buying at Auction*". I will save "*Buying at Auction*" for that next book.

What Is An Auction?

First, what is an *Auction*? One very basic definition is that an Auction is:

A Method of Selling
That Unites Buyers & Sellers in a Public Gathering
To Help Determine Fair Market Value
By Selling Goods In A Competitive Bidding Situation.

Let's take a look at this definition and break it down.

A Method of Selling: First, Auctions are a "*Method of Selling*". Most have heard of the "*Retail Method of Selling*" and the "*Wholesale Method of Selling*". Auctions are simply a different approach to selling *Personal Property*.

That Unites Buyers & Sellers in a Public Gathering: Both retail transactions and wholesale transactions can theoretically be accomplished with only two people...the *Seller* and the *Buyer*. Auctions required a minimum of three people to work effectively: the *Auctioneer*, and at least *two Bidders*. The more bidders, the more effective the Auction will be. Hence, Auctions work best in a *Public Gathering* with multiple potential bidders.

To Help Determine Fair Market Value: In both the *Retail* and *Wholesale* methods of selling, the "*Seller*" sets the asking price, and the "*Buyer*" has the option of either accepting the seller's asking price, negotiating a lower selling price, or rejecting the selling price. With Auctions, the buyers set Fair Market Value by what they are willing to bid.

By Selling Goods in a Competitive Bidding Situation. In an Auction, the Auctioneer simply asks for a starting price, and once that starting price is achieved, continues soliciting increasing bids from all interested potential bidders. The competitive bidding stops when no one else is willing to bid any higher, and the highest bidder represents the winning bidder.

In theory then, the highest competitive bid represents *Fair Market Value*, on that given day, for that given item, at that given location.

What Is An Auctioneer?

One definition I have heard is that an Auctioneer is:

A Personal Property Professional
Specializing In High Speed, Rapidly Increasing,
Verbal Numerical Techniques

When we're done with this chapter I think you will agree that there is a whole lot more to being a successful Auctioneer than simply talking fast.

Auctioneers Are Not All The Same

One very basic premise that many people fail to understand is that "*Auctioneers are not all the same*". I can't tell you how many people locate an Auctioneer by opening up the Yellow Pages and calling the first Auctioneer they find. That makes about as much sense as opening up the Yellow Pages and calling the first doctor that you see, without first determining what that doctor's area of specialty is.

In the most simplistic of terms, there are three types of Auctioneers:

- *Full-Service Auctioneers*. These Auctioneers sell all types of merchandise, specializing in households and estate situations. Although most have an expertise in one or more specialty areas, they have a general understanding in almost all types of merchandise. They understand how to put a successful Auction together, and they understand how to organize, advertise, and pull-off a successful Auction. But most importantly, they have a following of bidders that are interested in purchasing a wide variety of merchandise. Without a strong following of potential buyers, an Auctioneer is useless to you.

- *Specialty Auctioneers*: These Auctioneers specialize in selling a specific type of merchandise. It could be Antiques, Collectibles, Automobiles, Books, Jewelry, Art, whatever. They are often experts within their area of expertise, but may not have broad market knowledge in areas outside their areas of specialty. And if you have a specific type of merchandise, you will need to locate the most appropriate specialty Auctioneer to sell that merchandise. The local Doll Auctioneer may be the nicest Auctioneer around, but if you ask that Auctioneer to sell your tool collection, they most likely will have neither the expertise needed to sell tools, nor the following of potential buyers who are interested in buying your tools.

The Professional Bid Caller...These Auctioneers are the hired guns who have an excellent Auction chant and who can basically sell anything. They sell their Auction services to companies such as Auto Auctions, and they earn their pay by selling large quantities of merchandise, for top dollar, in the shortest amount of time. Just keep in mind that although these Auctioneers may be excellent bid callers, they may or may not have the expertise, organizational strength, marketing ability, or following of potential bidders to effectively sell the types of merchandise that you have.

We'll talk more about how to locate the right Auctioneer for your personal situation later in this chapter.

What's the Difference Between an Auctioneer and Auction House? An *Auctioneer* is an individual who sells items at Auction. Most Auctioneers work alone, either as *Full Service Auctioneers*, *Specialty Auctioneers*, or *Professional Bid Callers*. They are the individuals who call the sale. There are thousands of Auctioneers throughout the United States. I am one of them.

An *Auction House* or *Auction Company* is a non-person. It is a business entity whose primary business is to sell things at Auction. An *Auction House* employs individual *Auctioneers* whose primary job is selling things at *Auction* for the *Auction House*.

Auctioneer and Auction House Licensing and Bonding: This is an area that few outside the Auction Industry understand. And it is an extremely important question that potential consignors almost always fail to ask.

Because Auctioneers handle people's *Personal Property* assets, and thereby frequently handle large amounts of their money, certain states require that Auctioneers be licensed and bonded in their state. This is intended to protect residents of their state against illegal and fraudulent Auction practices by any Auctioneer operating within that state. I live in Pennsylvania, and our state requires that each Auctioneer, and each Auction House doing business in our state, be both licensed and bonded in order to conduct Auction business in our state.

As a matter of fact, oversight of the Auction business in Pennsylvania is even more stringent than that. In order to become an Auctioneer in Pennsylvania, prospective Auctioneers must:

- Serve an apprenticeship under a state-licensed Auctioneer for a period of at least two years.
- They must be state-licensed as an *"Apprentice Auctioneer"* during their apprenticeship.
- Prior to becoming a state-licensed Auctioneer they must pass a written Auctioneer examination that is given by the state.
- They must carry a legal bond that meets the minimum set by the state.
- Or, they must attended a six-month Auctioneering course offered at one of two area community colleges in Pennsylvania, and then pass the written state test and purchase the required bond.

If anyone has a problem with a Pennsylvania Auctioneer, they have the right to appear before the *Pennsylvania Board of Auctioneers* in our state capital of Harrisburg. This board consists of several Auctioneers, and several non-Auctioneers. Their role is to hear any complaint filed against any Auctioneer, and when appropriate, either rule in favor of the Auctioneer, fine the Auctioneer for their misdeeds, or suspend or revoke the Auctioneer's license to do business within the state of Pennsylvania.

Across the Delaware River in the state of New Jersey, there is no Auctioneer licensing law, there is no bonding requirement, and there is no New Jersey State Board of Auctioneers to hear consumer complaints. In theory, an individual in New Jersey could be released from prison today, and legally call an Auction in New Jersey on the same day.

In which state would you feel more comfortable hiring an Auctioneer to sell your *Personal Property* and handle your money?

HOME DOWNSIZING TIP: Before hiring an Auctioneer, ask them if they are legally licensed by their state, and if they have ever had any complaints filed against them for illegal or fraudulent Auction practices. If you don't ask the question, they will never volunteer the information.

Why Do People Sell at Auction?

There are many reasons people who are downsizing consign their Personal Property to Auction.

- It's a fast and easy way to dispose of excess *Personal Property.*
- It can be accomplished quickly.
- If offers Fair Market Value.
- The expense can be quite reasonable.
- To raise cash for nearly any reason.
- In the hope of making a profit.
- To create space in their home or business.
- To eliminate un-needed excess *Personal Property.*
- To sell *Personal Property* that may be difficult to sell in any other way.
- To place a value on items that you are uncertain what to charge privately.

- To avoid a potential fight between friends or family members. Let the highest bidder take it home.

What Can Be Sold At Auction?

Pretty much anything can be sold at Auction.

- *Antiques*: Furniture, Jewelry, Decorative Accessories, Primitives, etc.
- *Collectibles*: Coins, Stamps, Books, Postcards, China & Glassware, Dolls, Memorabilia, etc.
- *Leisure Items*: Camping Supplies, Boats, Canoes, Jet Skis, Sporting Goods, etc.
- *Real Estate*: Single Family Homes, Condominiums, Townhouses, Land, Commercial Real Estate, Warehouses, etc.
- *Household Items*: Used Furniture, Appliances, Refrigerators, Freezers, Washers, Dryers, Electrical Goods, Stereos, Televisions, Videos, Clothing, Carpets, Beds & Bedding, Garden Tools & Equipment, etc.
- *Food & Consumables*: Food, Wines, Spirits, Beers, etc. (subject to certain legal limitations)
- *Office Equipment*: Desks, Chairs, Filing Cabinets, Electronics & Telecommunication Equipment, etc.
- *Computer Equipment*: Desktop Computers, Laptop Computers, Monitors, Printers, Scanners, Modems, etc.
- *Motor Vehicles*: Cars, Vans & Trucks, Motorcycles, Airplanes, Recreational Vehicles, Antique Vehicles, Automobile Parts, etc.
- *Industrial Plant & Machinery*: Plant Equipment & Machinery, Hand Tools, Surplus Inventory, Scrap Material, etc.
- *Agricultural*: Buildings, Machinery, Tools, Crops, Livestock, Vehicles, etc.
- *Government*: Armed Forces Surplus, Government Surplus, Seized & Confiscated Goods; etc.

Five Different Auction Formats

Should you decide to sell any of your *Personal Property* at Auction, you will most likely see one of the following five Auction formats used.

- *Ascending Bid Auctions*: Also known as *English Auctions*, this Auction format is without doubt the most common form of Auction used in the United States today. In *Ascending Bid Auctions* the Auctioneer opens the bidding at a specific price, and keeps soliciting ascending or increasing bids from all interested bidders until the bidding stops. At that point the highest bidder is the winning bidder. In this format Auction participants bid openly against one another, and at least two bidders are required for this type of Auction to work (unless a Reserve is involved, which we'll discuss shortly). *Ascending Bid Auctions* will most likely be the type of Auction used to sell your *Personal Property*.

- *Descending Bid Auctions*: Also known as *Dutch Auctions,* under this Auction format the Auctioneer starts the bidding with a high asking price, and then lowers the bidding in a descending format until one bidder accepts the Auctioneer's price. The first bidder to accept the Auctioneer's bid is the winning bidder. This Auction format is sometimes called a *"Dutch Auction"* because it is the format used in Dutch Tulip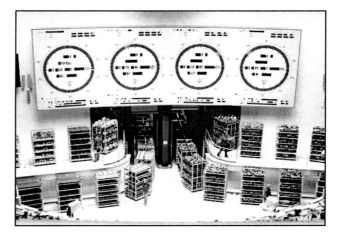
Auctions. (Note that this "*Dutch Auction*" format should not be confused with what eBay calls a *Dutch Auction,* which is used to describe online Auctions where identical goods are offer simultaneously.) In theory, the advantage of the *"Dutch"* Auction format is that the winning bidder can opt to take all or most of a specific commodity at that winning price, thereby preventing their competition from buying anything that day. In practice, however, *Descending Bid Auctions* are rarely used in the United States.

- *Silent Auctions*: These are a variation of the *Ascending Bid Auctions* except that instead of verbal bidding led by an Auctioneer, ascending bids are written on a sheet of paper. At the pre-defined end of the Auction the highest listed bidder wins the item. *Silent Auctions* are often used in charity events, with many items auctioned simultaneously with a common finish time. The Auction is "*Silent*" in that there is no Auctioneer. The winning bidder pays the highest price they wrote on the bid form. If you donate any of your *Personal Property* to a favorite group or charity, some of your items may be sold in the *Silent Auction* format.

- *Sealed Bid Auctions*, In this type of Auction all bidders must submit their maximum bids in a sealed envelope, in the approved manner, by a pre-announced Auction deadline. At this point no bidder knows the bid of any other bidder. At a pre-announced time all of the envelopes are opened with the highest bidder being the winning bidder, provided of course the minimum or reserve price is reached. The highest bidder pays the price they submitted. Bidders can only submit one bid, and they cannot adjust their bid based upon what their competition is bidding. These Auctions are more often used in selling government property, although we have occasionally seen entire collections sold in this manner.

- *Internet Auctions*: This Auction format is the most recent, and has actually only come into being over the past ten years. Although eBay is the most common form of Internet Auction, you should be aware that there are hundreds of different Internet Auctions, catering to specific customers and specialties. Because there are so many Internet Auctions going on in cyberspace, you just need to understand that depending upon what you are selling, this could be a selling option you may want to explore in more detail.

Reserve and Absolute Auctions

Basically there are two types of Auctions.

- *Auction with Reserve*: These Auctions allow consignors to sell with a *Minimum Selling Price*, which is sometimes called a *Reserve Price*. If the bidding does not reach the minimum or reserve price, the item will not sell and the consignor retains title to it.

- *Auctions without Reserve*: More commonly called "*Absolute Auctions*", these are Auctions without a minimum or reserve price. In *Absolute Auctions* the highest bidder is the winning bidder, regardless of the final selling price, and title to the merchandise is transferred when the Auctioneer says "*Sold*", whether the consignor is happy with the selling price or not.

Considering that the *Uniform Commercial Code* states that all Auctions shall be considered "*With Reserve*" unless stated otherwise, why in the world would anyone want to risk their merchandise selling at *Absolute Auction* when they could protect themselves with a reserve? I hear this question all the time, and frankly I consider it to be the #1 obstacle to people consigning to Public Auction.

Believe it or not, there is a very good answer to this question, and it is predicated upon the very premise that makes the Auction process work. You need to understand that regardless of who the Auctioneer is, where the Auction is taking place, or what the merchandise is, the primary reason bidders go to an Auction is in the pursuit of a bargain. If they wanted to pay retail price, they could go to a retail store and buy something off the shelf. No, people go to Auctions looking for bargains. And if prospective bidders knew that everything in an Auction was being sold with a reserve, they wouldn't bother going to that Auction. And without bidders, you don't have an Auction. It's as simple as that.

Most Auctioneers use *Absolute Auction* in order to attract the greatest number of prospective bidders to an Auction. And once the bidders are at the Auction, let the bidding begin. The more bidders who attend an Auction, generally the higher the prices because of the heightened bidding competition.

This contrasts with a *Reserve Auction*, where the item for sale may not be sold if the final bid is not high enough to satisfy the seller. Although a *Reserve Auctions* may generally be considered safer by the seller than an Absolute *Auction*, *Reserve Auctions* generally result in a lower final price due primarily to the decreased bidding competition.

This doesn't mean that Auctioneers never use reserves. They do. Rather it means that reserves are generally implemented only for certain types of merchandise, and only in certain situations. Many Auctioneers will be willing to accept a reserve on a high value item, where the consignor's potential risk could be great. In these instances, many Auctioneers will accept what they perceive as a "*Reasonable Reserve*", with "*reasonable*" generally meaning that even with the reserve, that item will most likely sell to the highest bidder. However, you should understand that if you and the Auctioneer agree to a reserve price, and if that reserve price is not met, you may have to pay the Auctioneer a commission based upon that reserve price. This is called a "*Buy-In*" fee.

114

Four Auction Formats

There are four different Auctions formats and, depending upon the type of merchandise you are selling, it will generally be sold in one of these four formats.

- *Non-Catalog Auctions*: Different Auctioneers have different names for these Auctions, such *Estate Auctions* or *Consignment Auctions*, but this is generally the most common type of Auction to be found. This is where the general merchandise is sold. It could be pots and pans, box lots, furniture, art, smalls, and decorative accessories. Some Auctioneers have these Auctions weekly, other Auctioneers less frequently. But the objective of these Auctions is to sell the merchandise quickly without the added expense of storing and handling it again. Consignors bring it in the back door, and winning bidders take it out the front door. This is the type of Auction where most of your *Personal Property* will be sold. Rarely is merchandise in these Auctions sold with a reserve.

- *Catalog Auctions*: This is generally the most preferred type of Auction, but don't expect much of your merchandise to end up here. This type of Auction is reserved only for the best-of-the-best merchandise. In Catalog Auctions the best merchandise is held back for a later Auction. This merchandise is photographed and pictured in a slick Auction Catalog. This is the high-end and highly desirable merchandise that warrants the additional handling and storage, and this type of merchandise is often sold with a reserve.

- *Specialty Auctions*: These are Auctions where all of the merchandise is similar in nature, such as Hummel Auctions, Coin Auctions, Doll Auctions, etc. Sometimes they are single owner Specialty Auctions; usually they are multi-consignor Auctions.

- *Internet Auctions*: These are the most recent type of Auction, and are limited to a specific type of merchandise. These Auctions are reserved for merchandise which will do better on a national or international stage. Selling such merchandise on the Internet enables you to reach the largest potential pool of bidders, and thereby most likely achieve the best selling price. *Non-Catalog, Catalog Auction*, and *Specialty Auction* items can be sold in an *Internet Auction* format. Merchandise which generally sells best on the Internet would include:
    - The rarest and best items.
    - Items with a recognizable name.
    - Those items having a broad appeal.
    - Items without any condition issues.
    - Items which are easily describable.
    - Items which are shippable.

Where Would You Prefer To Have Your Personal Property Sold?

This is a question that I ask potential consignors all the time. There are three different locations where Auctions are held, and depending upon the Auctioneer you select, you might be able to have your merchandise sold at one of these locations.

- *On Site Auctions*: Sometimes called *"Premises Auctions"*, these are Auctions that are held at your home or business and the bidders come to you. Occasionally these represent the preferred type of Auction. Nothing has to be moved. People come to your home. It is sold right there, on your front lawn or under your roof, without incurring any moving expenses. For some, this is the perfect option...*unless it rains or storms, or if the temperature is either too hot or too cold.* In reality it normally has to be nearly an ideal setting for an On-Site Auction to work perfectly. In a normal situation, all of the following are required in order to have a successful On-Site Auction:

  - o   The right merchandise.
  - o   Sufficient grounds to display the merchandise.
  - o   Ample parking.
  - o   Acceptable zoning.
  - o   The owner must normally pay all expenses, including:
    - ▪   Advertising
    - ▪   Staffing
    - ▪   Tent
    - ▪   Port-A-Johns
    - ▪   Etc.
  - o   And the weather must cooperate.

- *Rented Auction Facility*: Smaller Auctioneers who don't own their own Auction Center typically rent a facility on a short-term basis. This could include a Church Hall, Hotel Banquet Facility, Firehouse, Convention Center, or similar location.

- *Auction House*: Larger Auction Companies typically have their own *Auction Centers*. Sometimes they are simply *Auction Barns*, other times they are state-of-the-art *Auction Houses*.

On-Site Auction, Rented Auction Facility, or Auction House...where do you want your *Personal Property* sold? It's your call.

The Role of the Traditional Auctioneer

The Auction Business has been around for centuries, and the business has changed very little...*until recently*. Over the centuries the role of the traditional Auctioneer was simply to:
- Obtain the Merchandise.
- Sign the Contract.
- Advertise it.
- Sell it on location.
- Locate enough new merchandise to hold the next Auction.

This was it. And this is the way that many Auctioneers are still running their businesses today. Many remain small time Auctioneers who have yet to embrace today's changing technology. But other Auctioneers are changing with the times and, depending upon the types of *Personal Property* you are selling, you may want to seek out an Auctioneer who is keeping up with the times, and hopefully is even ahead of the curve.

What You Should Be Looking For In An Auctioneer Today

The Auction business is changing and you should be looking for the best Auctioneer to handle your needs. Some areas you should consider include:

- *Absentee Bidding*: Does the Auctioneer accept Absentee Bids? People today are busier than ever and few have time to spend an entire day at an Auction waiting for only one or two items to be sold. Absentee Bids will make you more money. If your prospective Auctioneer does not accept Absentee Bids, my advice is to find an Auctioneer that does.

- *Telephone Bidding*: Dittos on Telephone Bidding. If your prospective Auctioneer does not accept Telephone Bids, my advice is to find one that does.

- *Cell Phones and WiFi Computers*: With increasing frequency bidders are calling prospective buyers of merchandise to gauge their level of interest...*before they bid on it*...using their cell phones. And an increasing number of customers are bringing their wireless computers to Auctions, using wireless connections to access eBay or other selling venues to help them decide what they should pay for certain merchandise before bidding on it. If your prospective Auctioneer does not provide cell phone and WiFi capabilities, find one that does.

- *E-Mail & Digital Images*: This has changed the way Auctions do business. We recently had two acorn clocks pictured on our web site. A prospective bidder from Tasmania (near Australia) e-mailed, indicating that he was a serious potential bidder and requesting better photographs. We took the digital images, sent them to him within 10 minutes, and almost immediately he e-mailed back with two bids of

117

ten times what we originally expected to get for those clocks. Can you calculate how long it would have taken us to take 35mm photos, have them developed, and then send them to Tasmania, only 10 years ago. If your prospective Auctioneer does not use eMail or digital images, find one that does.

- *Expect Greater Reliance on Web Sites and Internet Advertising*: As the costs of traditional advertising continue to increase, many Auctioneers are reducing the amount of their space advertising, and directing people to their web sites where they can list more text, and use more photos, than through the more traditional advertising outlets. This is absolutely vital in today's Auction world. If your prospective Auctioneer does not have a web site, and a good web site at that, find one that does.

- *E-Mail Blasts*: Some Auctions send out a periodic E-Mail Blasts to their customers, informing them of what is coming up in their future Auctions. This could mean free advertising for your merchandise. If your prospective Auctioneer does not use E-Mail Blasts to promote your merchandise, find one that does.

- *Auction Zip*: www.AuctionZip.com is a fairly new Web Site that promotes Auctions. And many people are now going to *Auction Zip* before turning to the more traditional Auction advertising sources because *Auction Zip* covers so many different Auctions. You simply go to their Search Function, key in what you are looking for (e.g., *Maxfield Parrish, Depression Glass, Roseville Pottery,* etc.), and *Auction Zip* will direct you to any Auctions in their system which are selling that specific merchandise. If your prospective Auction doesn't use *Auction Zip*, find one that does.

- *eBay Live and Internet Auctions*: This is the most important thing to you. You want your merchandise sold on the Internet where possible. When you have floor bidders competing against Internet bidders for your merchandise, you have the best of all worlds. If you have higher-end merchandise, and if your prospective Auctioneer doesn't utilize Internet Auctions, my advice would be to find one who does.

How Does The Auction Consignment Process Work?

This is probably the most important part of this chapter because this is where we will try to bring all of the concepts put forth in this chapter together for you.

- *Locate the Right Auctioneer*: There are many Auctioneers out there. Some are better, some are more professional, some are more honest, than others. Find an Auctioneer who has an excellent reputation and one you that you are comfortable with.

- *Study Their Terms & Conditions of Sale*: Ask for a copy of their Auction Contract ahead of time. Study it closely, and take it to any attorney or other counsel if necessary. Ask questions of the Auctioneer where appropriate.

- *Get It in Writing*: Request an Auction Contract that spells out the Terms, Conditions, and Commissions that will be involved in selling your merchandise. If that Auctioneer won't give it to you in writing, walk away and find another Auctioneer. A handshake agreement is worth nothing in court.

- *Schedule an Auction Date.*

- *Schedule a Delivery or Pick-Up Date.*

- *Confirm When You Will Be Paid.*

Questions You Should Ask Any Auctioneer Before You Consign

Ask these questions. You have the right to ask questions. And if you fail to ask them, you will never get the answers to them.

- *How Long in Business.* How long has the Auctioneer been in business? Do you want to be the first client of a new Auctioneer who has never conducted their own Auction, who is fresh out of Auction School, and who does not yet have a strong following?
- *Licensed & Bonded.* Is the Auctioneer licensed and bonded? Some states require it, others don't. Would you feel more comfortable dealing with an Auctioneer who is licensed and bonded?

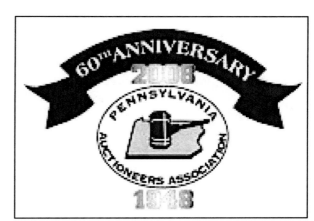

- *Formal Complaints Filed Against Them.* Have any formal complaints ever been filed against the Auctioneer? If so, what are the details? Where they exonerated, were they fined? Or even worse, was their license suspended or revoked?
- *Professional Associations.* Are they members of any professional Auctioneer or Appraisal Associations? For how long? Had they ever held leadership positions within these organizations?
- *Professional Honors.* Have they received any professional designations, awards, or honors that distinguish them from their peers?
- *Auction Date and Location.* When will the Auction of your merchandise be held? Where will it be held?
- *Storage.* Where will your merchandise be stored until it is sold? In a secure, climate-controlled building. Or in a freezing trailer or storage locker? What is the security like?
- *Insurance.* Is your merchandise insured while in the Auctioneer's possession? For how much? If it is a blanket amount of coverage, what happens if a single piece is damaged, lost, or stolen? How long will it take to get paid for the lost item(s)? How much does the Insurance cost?
- *Marketing & Advertising.* How will your consignment be advertised and marketed? Will it be photographed? Any there special charges for this?
- *Absentee & Telephone Bids.* Does the Auctioneer accept Absentee and/or Telephone Bids? If not, it will cost you money.
- *Moving Expense.* Is the Auctioneer picking up the merchandise? If so, how much will it cost? A flat amount or hourly rate? If an hourly rate, only the time there, or point-to-point?
- *Packing Expense.* Are you packing or are they? What is the packing fee?

- *Moving and Packing Insurance*. What are the limitations? What are the costs?
- *When Will You Get Paid*. Beware! Some Auctions pay quickly; others won't pay you for six months or more. The payment date should be specified, in writing, in the Auction Contract.

And the last question should be....

- *What is the Commission Rate?*

This is almost always the first question I am asked, but in my opinion, it should be the last question asked. Why? Because the lowest commission doesn't necessarily correlate to the best Auctioneer. As a matter of fact, it is usually just the opposite. It is often those Auctioneers who have a hard time attracting consignors who must cut their commission, just in order to get the job.

Remember how we started out this chapter..."*Auctioneers are not all the same*". You get what you pay for. I'm not suggesting that you don't pay attention to commission. And I'm not suggesting that you don't ask the commission question. Rather, I am suggesting that you ask the other questions first. And then, once you are satisfied that you have found the right Auctioneer, ask what the commission rate will be.

How Do Auctioneers Charge For Their Services

There are several different ways Auctioneers charge for their services
- *Commission*: Nearly every Auctioneer is going to charge you a commission. That commission is typically either a flat percentage of the final selling price, or a sliding commission scale. If the *Flat Rate Commission* is 25%, and the final selling price is $1,000, you will receive $750 from the sale of that item. If the *Sliding Scale Commission* is 25% of the first $500, and 10% of anything above $500, you would receive $825 ($125 on the first $500, and $50 on the amount over $500, or a total commission of $175).

- *Buyer's Premium*: The *Buyer's Premium* is an additional fee that most Auction Companies charge the buyer today. If the *Buyer's Premium* is 10%, and the final selling price is $1,000, the buyer pays the Auctioneer $1,100.

- *Additional Charges*: Some Auctioneers charge an additional amount for such services as:
  - o Packing & Moving
  - o Photography
  - o Catalog Listings
  - o Cleaning
  - o Special Handling
  - o Etc.

Commissions: Commissions can vary widely, depending upon the Auctioneer, location, and type and condition of the merchandise being consigned. *Flat Rate Commissions* are generally more common than *Sliding Scale Commissions*.

Are commissions negotiable? Perhaps, depending upon the Auction House and what you are consigning. Expect little or no negotiation on common or general merchandise. However, if you have something special, such as a $100,000+ painting, the major Auction Houses will often work on a smaller commission basis, using the *Buyer's Premium* as their financial incentive. And on the best-of-the-best merchandise, some consignors have negotiated interest-free advances against the final selling price. But this is extremely rare, and generally limited to only a few of the major international Auction Companies who have the means to do so.

Buyer's Premium

Why on earth are buyers willing to pay the Auction Company a *"Premium"* of 10%-25% over the final selling price of an item? *"Well, at least it's not coming out of my money?"* is the most common remark from novice sellers.

We'll address both thoughts shortly, but first let's address the *Buyer's Premium*. First, where did the *Buyer's Premium* originate? It started with the major New York Auction Houses. In years past Auction Houses raised their seller commissions whenever expenses started catching up with revenues. However, circa 1980 the major New York Auction Houses realized that if they kept their commission the same, and passed the *"commission"* increase along to the buyer, it would give them a huge advantage in acquiring consignments.

Consider it this way: Auction Company "A" is going charge you a 25% commission, while Auction Company "B is only going to charge you a 15% commission, while passing along a *"10% Buyer's Premium"* to the buyer. Who are you going to consign with? Of course the Auction House with the lowest commission The Auction Company is still making the same amount, but the perception to the consignor is that they are paying a lower commission.

Another reality of the Auction business is that the bidders (hence, the money) go to the Auctioneer who has the best merchandise. And in order to acquire the best merchandise in order to compete, more Auctioneers were forced to resort to the *Buyer's Premium*. Many Auctioneers tried to resist the Buyer's Premium, and certain buyers tried to boycott Auctions Companies that went to the *"Buyer's Penalty"*. But the boycotts failed, and the *Buyer's Premium* remains as strong today as ever.

Why are buyers willing to pay the *Buyer's Premium*? Because most buyers don't perceive it to be an additional penalty or cost, they view it simply as part of the cost of the merchandise. If they are willing to pay $1,000 for an item at Auction, and there is a 20% Buyer's Premium in effect, that bidder will only bid up to $800, and with the 20% Buyer's Premium, their true cost is still around $1,000.

Whether you accept the Buyer's Premium or not, as a potential Auction seller, you needed to understand the concept of the *Buyer's Premium*, and how it will impact you, before consigning to Auction.

How Does Someone Bid At Auction?

As mentioned earlier, my goal in this chapter is not necessarily intended to explain how to buy at Auction, but rather how to sell at Auction. Therefore I will just take this very limited section to explain to you how someone bids and buys at Auction.

- *Register To Obtain A Bidding Number*: You must first be registered and have a bidding number in order to bid. When registering you will normally be asked to provide a picture ID which includes your name, address and contact information. This is so the Auctioneer can stay in contact with you (e.g., notifying you of future Auctions), as well as locate you if necessary (e.g., if you bounce a check or walk out without paying).

- *Inspection or Preview Period*: Prior to the start of the Auction is the *"Preview"* or *"Inspection"* period. This is the time where you can hold, touch, feel, and see everything in the Auction prior to bidding on it. Most items at Auction are sold *"As Is-Where Is"*. That means once you buy it, you own it. The Auction Company will not take it back, under any circumstances, even if it was broken when you purchased it. So you had better check it out prior to bidding on it.

- *Terms & Conditions of Sale*: Before bidding you must read and understand the Auctioneer's *Terms and Conditions of Sale*. Auctioneers have varying terms & conditions and you had better understand what the rules of the game are...*before you place your first bid. Terms & Conditions of Sale* will include such items as:
    o Acceptable methods of payment.
    o Buyer's Premium.
    o When you become responsible for what you bought.
    o When something can be returned.
    o Etc.

- *The Auction Starts and Sales Are Recorded*: As each item is sold, three pieces of information are recorded by the Auction Clerk. Usually this is done through a computer clerking system, but occasionally manual hand-clerked tickets are still used by a few Auctioneers:
    o *Consignor #*: Each consignor in the Auction has a unique code and each item in the Auction is marked with the specific consignor's number. This is how the Auction Company keeps track of what they owe each consignor.
    o *Winning Bidder #*: Each bidder at an Auction also has a unique Bidder number, and whenever they purchase something at the Auction, their bidding number is recorded, along with the final sale price.
    o *Final Sale Price*: As each item is sold, the final sale price is recorded as well.

- *Check Out and Pay Your Bill*: Once you are ready to leave, you simply proceed to the check-out counter and present your bidder number. They will tally up what you owe them and, after you settle your account, you are welcome to go home with your merchandise.

What Doesn't Sell Well at Auction?

Auctions are a place where you can sell quality items in a competitive-bidding situation. They are not dumping grounds for all of the old merchandise that you no longer want or need. These items will generally not sell well at Auction:

- *Appliances*...unless they are newer and in perfect working condition.
- *Bed Pillows*...would you buy someone else's bed pillow at Auction?
- *Bicycles*...that are rusted or not in excellent working condition.
- *Built-In Dishwashers or Ovens*...If you send them and they fail to sell, expect to pay a disposal fee.
- *Canning Jars*...few people are still canning today.
- *Children's Car Seats*... unless less than 2 years old and in perfect condition. Would you place your grandchild in an *as-is* car seat?

- *Clothing*... that is not designer clothing, or unusual in nature and of excellent quality.
- *Computer Monitors*...unless newer and flat screen.
- *Computers and/or Printers*...unless in excellent working condition with the latest operating systems.
- *Console TV's, Console Stereos, or TV/Radio/Stereo Combos.*
- *Curtains & Curtain Rods.*
- *Exercise Equipment.*
- *Electrical or Battery-Operated Items*...that are not technologically current and in excellent condition.
- *Encyclopedia Britannica*...or any other Encyclopedias.
- *Gas Grills*...unless they are current and state of the art.
- *Hospital or Adjustable Beds.*
- *Jig Saw Puzzles*... that are opened or missing pieces.
- *Metal Desks and Metal Filing Cabinets*...dittos on the probable disposal fee.
- *Microwaves*...that are not state of the art technologically and in excellent working order.
- *Paint Cans*...that are opened, used, or outdated.
- *Plastic Coffee Mugs, Cups or Glasses.*
- *Pots and Pans*...that are not in clean and attractive condition.
- *Skis, Poles, Boots, and Snow Boards*... that are not state of the art.
- *Upholstered Sofas, Love Seats, and Chairs*...unless in almost new and unblemished condition.
- *Stuffed Animals*...unless newer, clean, and with tags.
- *Typewriters*...either electric or manual, unless they are of the vintage Antique models.
- *Washers, Dryers, Refrigerators, Freezers*...or any larger appliance that is more than a few years old, in blemished condition, or not in excellent working condition.

Definition of a Successful Auctioneer

The best definition of a successful Auctioneer that I ever heard was this:

A Successful Auctioneer Bring Two Parties Together

Sellers...Who Want To Receive As Much As Possible, and

Buyers...Who Want To Pay As Little As Possible

...Into A Situation Where Both Sides Walk Away Happy.

* * * * *

Auction Advantages
- Auction offers Fair Market Value.
- Auctions enable you to sell a large quantity of merchandise in a short period of time.
- You can have a check in hand within 3-4 weeks (and sometimes sooner) after you deliver your merchandise to the Auction House.
- Within certain parameters you can schedule when your merchandise will be sold.
- Most types of *Personal Property* can be sold at Auction.
- Your merchandise will sell in a competitive bidding situation, and competition among bidders will stimulate prices and establish current market value.
- Auctions can eliminate the appearance of any closed-door transaction.
- Some things may sell for even more than they are worth.

Auction Disadvantages
- Not all Auctioneers are good Auctioneers. You will have to locate the right Auctioneer for what you are selling.
- You'll have to pay commissions & other expenses.
- You'll either have to move it to Auction, or pay someone to move it for you.
- Generally you will have to sell at Absolute Auction without minimum or reserve.
- Some things will sell for less than they are worth.
- Once it's gone, its gone, regardless of the selling price.

Home Downsizing Tips

✓ Auctions represent an efficient, quick, and easy way to convert your household items and Personal Property assets into cash.

✓ Visit a prospective Auction House during an Auction day, un-announced, and see if you feel comfortable with their process, staff, Auctioneers, parking, and overall demeanor. Trust your instincts. Either if it feels right, or if it feels wrong.

✓ Auctions create competitive bidding among bidders which stimulates prices and helps to establish fair market value.

✓ Auctions take place in the public view. By consigning to a reputable Auction House you can avoid the potential impression of any closed-door transaction.

✓ Many Auction Houses will pay you within one month of the Auction date, which allows you to better plan your cash flow. The payment date should be clearly specified in your Auction Contract.

✓ If you must pay to move your merchandise to Auction, generally expect that you will see very little of the first $1,000 in Gross Sales after paying commission and moving expense.

✓ Closely read, and understand, the Auctioneer's *Terms and Conditions of Sale...before, not after...*you sign the Auction Contract.

NOTE: For a complete listing of *Auction Definitions and Terminology*, see Chapter 24: *Home Downsizing Resources.*

*D*ispose of All Excess Items

This is where it all comes together. What's the best way to dispose of your *Personal Property Assets*? In Chapters 18-19 we'll help you to wrap things up.

✓ *Creating a Plan of Action:* Remember that the ultimate goal of the *Home Downsizing* process is to dispose of your excess, unwanted, and un-needed *Personal Property*. And with so much for you to do, a *Plan of Action* makes it easier to understand where you have been, and what you must still do, in order to reach your goal of a downsized home. In this section we will help you to prepare your *Plan of Auction*.

✓ *We'll Show You How to Execute Your Plan of Action:* This is the time you begin to turn your excess *Personal Property* assets into cash. It's now time to begin disposing.

✓ *We'll Help You Create a Disposition Schedule*: Most of you will utilize more than one of the selling options we have just discussed so the best way to proceed from here is to build a *Disposition Schedule* into your *Plan of Action*. This will provide you with a more precise, step-by-step approach to getting it all done.

✓ *We'll Make Some Final Recommendations*: In these chapters we'll be making some additional recommendations and offering some additional *Home Downsizing Tips* that should make this process even easier.

Chapter 18

Setting a Plan of Action

This will be a short chapter because you are nearly done. In *AVID Steps #1 - #2 - #3* we started the *Home Downsizing* process moving forward:

- We've *identified* your Personal Property Assets.
- We've *identified* what you want to keep for your next home or next phase in life.
- We've *identified* what you want to give to family and friends.
- We've *identified* major items you want to donate.
- We've *identified* what you want to sell.
- We've *identified* what needs to be disposed of.
- And we've *identified* ballpark values on what your *Personal Property* may be worth in today's market.

Now it's time to actually downsize. What's your *Plan of Action*? How should you proceed in order to finalize your individual *Home Downsizing*?

At this point different people will formulate different *Plans of Action*. There is no single best plan for everyone because each situation is different. The personalities involved in each situation are different, and have different needs. How you set your individual *Plan of Action* will depend upon several factors, including:
- What do you still have left to dispose of?
- Which selling options are best suited for you?
- What is your time frame?
- What is your individual situation?
- Are you doing it yourself, or is someone else doing it for you?

Based upon the *10 Sorting Categories* that we have already identified, you should already be well on your way to finalizing your *Plan of Action*.

- *Initial Dump*: You should have already identified any items that you, your family and friends, and probably no one else in the world will want. If not, do it now.

- *Keeping It*: You should have already identified what you are keeping for your move or next phase in life. At this point it should somehow be marked (colored coded sticker, inventory list, etc) or placed in a secure storage area so it will not accidentally get mixed in with the items that you will be disposing of. If not, do it now.

- *Family and Friends*: You should have already identified and marked what is going to family and friends. Some of it may be gone already. If not, identify and mark it now.

- *Donation of Major Items*: By now you should have already identified what major items you may be donating to museums, institutions, or other organizations of choice. You also should have started the legal and paperwork trail that is associated with such charitable donations. You may have already started or completed this. If not, identify those items you wish to donate and start the legal and paperwork trail now.

- *Selling Privately*: You should have already identified those things that you prefer to sell outright and privately. You should have also thought about who you will be selling it to, and for what price. It may already be gone. If not, identify those items, and make a list of prospective buyers and your asking price(s) now. Remember that with this option, there are no commissions, no uncertainties, and no delays. But you also know that the buyer will be making a profit on the transaction. If they are making a fair profit, that's okay. If they are making a huge profit, that may or may not be acceptable to you because they will be making that huge profit at your expense.

- *Selling on eBay or the Internet*: Some items will sell better on eBay or the Internet and you should have already identified those items. If you are going to list the items yourself, you can now begin considering your listing descriptions, starting prices, high & low estimates, and minimum reserve price (if you will have one) now. If you are going to have someone else list your items on eBay for you, you should be narrowing down your choice of that person or business now.

- *Public Auction:* Some items will sell better at Public Auction and you should have already identified those items. You should also have already considered which Auctioneer or Auction Company you are going to use, after considering the key factors that we discussed in Chapter 17. If not, start considering this now.

- *Garage Sale, Tag Sale or other Retail Venue*: This is pretty much the last dumping ground before the final cleanout step. By now you should know my opinion about Garage Sales. I hate them because most people don't understand *Personal Property* values and all too often give it away at Garage Sales for pennies on the dollar. However, if you have already done your homework and have identified the general value of things, if you have already made plans to dispose of your better items in the most appropriate venue, then I have less of a problem with Garage Sales. And frankly, a Garage Sale at this point is probably your last chance to obtain any value at all on your remaining merchandise, before having to dumpster it.

- *Minor Item Donations*. After the Garage Sale is over, certain items of value will just not sell. You can count on it. Rather than throwing them away, considering donating them to a good cause of your choice. These organizations are not looking for junk, but rather items that can be re-sold for a modest amount to help people, or things that can be used to help those in need. Whether you are doing it out of the goodness of your heart or looking for the tax write-off, don't overlook this step before proceeding to the tenth and final sorting category.

- *Cleanout Specialist or Dumpster*: The primary difference between these two options is *"Who does it"*? and *"How much will it cost"*?. The final decision in this step doesn't have to be made until you have executed your *Plan of Action*, and everything else is gone.

Once you have specified what will be going to each of these ten sorting categories, you will have completed your *Home Downsizing Plan of Action* and are now ready to *Execute* it.

Chapter 19

Crossing It Off the List: Executing Your Plan of Action.

Most of the work is done. The stage is set. Your ducks should be in order. Now is the time to move.

This chapter will focus on the *Plan of Action* that we created in Chapter 18. However, in this chapter we will be taking one final look at what you must do to execute that step. And once you are done, you will *"Cross It Off The List"*.

Let's review each of the 10 primary sorting categories that we have already identified, and discuss what you must do to finalize this step.

1) Initial Dump: You have already identified any items that neither you, nor your family and friends, and probably no one else in the world, would want. This should have been one of the first things that you did because by doing this you would have eliminated any valueless items and, more importantly, given yourself additional room in which to work. You may have put it by the curb, taken it to the local dump, or rented a dumpster. But this step should already be done. If not, do it now, before proceeding any farther.

But remember: *Never start this step without having someone knowledgeable in Personal Property review what you may be throwing away.*

✓ When you're done with this option...*Cross it off the list*.

HOME DOWNSIZING TIP: Never dump anything until you have an understanding of the general value of an item. All too often you could end-up dumping things that have considerably more value than you realize.

---

2) Keeping It: You should have already identified what you are keeping for your move or next phase in life. If you have any serious doubts about whether to keep it or dispose of it at this point, out advice is *"keep it for now"*. Once gone, you cannot get it back. You can always decide to dispose of it at a later date.

At this point it should be somehow identified (colored coded sticker, inventory list, etc) or placed in a secure storage area so it will not accidentally get mixed in with items that you will be disposing of. If not, do it now.

✓ When you're done with this option...*Cross it off the list.*

HOME DOWNSIZING TIP: Clearly identify those items that you will be keeping, and insure that they don't accidentally get mixed up with items that you are disposing of. All too often we have seen people frantically calling the Auction House looking for a *"keeper"* that they had accidentally mixed in with their Auction consignment. Once gone, you can never get it back.

3) Family and Friends: You should have already identified and marked what is going to family and friends. Some of it may be gone already. If not call your family, and call your friends, and ask them to pick up their designated items at their earliest convenience. If they hesitate about picking it up, don't be afraid to give them a deadline. If they want it badly enough they will find a way to retrieve it. Unless there is good cause, consider placing that item in one of the other categories if the item is not picked up by the deadline date.

✓ When you're done with this option...*Cross it off the list.*

HOME DOWNSIZING TIP: Don't be afraid to give family and friends a reasonable deadline for removing what they will be taking. If they seriously want what you have offered, they will find a way to accommodate your deadline.

4) Donation of Major Items: You should have already identified what you may be donating to museums, church groups, non-profits, or other organizations of choice. Has the item been accepted for donation? Some organizations can take forever in getting back to you about your donation. If the item has been accepted for donation, you should have already started the legal and paperwork trail that is associated with such donations. If not, contact your attorney or legal advisor and wrap it up. If there is any question about the donation at this point, consider placing that item in one of the other categories.

✓ When you're done with this option...*Cross it off the list.*

HOME DOWNSIZING TIP: Stay in close contact with your attorney and other advisors on this subject. Do not cross it off the list until they tell you everything is done.

5) Selling Privately: You should have already identified those things that you prefer to sell outright and privately. And you should have thought about whom you will be selling to, and for what price.

First, contact the top three potential buyers, and ask each for a *"Firm Offer Price"* (an offer that they are serious about, and will not walk out on). Tell them that you will get back to them on their offer by a specific date.

Once you have more than one firm offer, contact your #1 preferred buyer and confirm that you can finalize a workable deal. If that deal falls through (as they often do), you can always call the #2 preferred buyer on your list. And if all private deals fall through (as they sometimes do), you can consider placing these items in another *Plan of Action* disposition category. However, if you obtain multiple price quotes, be considerate and respond to each private party, by the specified date that you set, and let them know your decision.

> ✓ Once you have been paid and the item(s) are gone, you're done with this
> option...*Cross it off the list*.

HOME DOWNSIZING TIP: When selling items privately, especially larger collections, be certain to get several *"Firm Price Quotes"*. You may be surprised at the wide range of offers that you receive.

6) Selling on eBay or the Internet: Some, but not all, items may sell better on eBay or the Internet, and you should have already identified those items. If you are going to list the items yourself, you can begin considering your listing descriptions now. Remember from Chapter 13 that it takes a considerable amount of work selling items on eBay. In our experience it can average nearly one hour per lot so get started early.

If you are going to have someone else list your items on eBay, you should be finalizing your choice of that person or business now. (See Chapter 14).

If any items fail to sell on eBay, you can either re-list them, or place them in any of the other remaining disposition categories.

> ✓ Once you have been paid and all eBay transactions are completed, you're done with
> this option...*Cross it off the list*.

HOME DOWNSIZING TIP: If selling on eBay, don't cross it off the list until positive feedback has been left by the buyer. Unfortunately, all too many items are returned by eBay buyers due to dissatisfaction with condition or some other factor.

7) Public Auction: Some, but not all, items may sell better at Public Auction and you should have already identified those items. This may include items that are too large to ship (e.g., furniture), items with condition issues (damaged or blemished merchandise), or items that have little buyer interest on eBay. It could also include your best merchandise, especially those

rarest pieces in the best condition,that could do exceptionally well if sold in a competitive bidding situation.

You should have also already considered which Auctioneer or Auction Company you are going to use, after considering the key factors we discussed in Chapter 17. If not, finalize this decision now.

Once you have decided what to send to Auction, and which Auction Company you will be using, contact that Auction Company to schedule a delivery date and Auction date for your items, but only after understanding their *Terms and Conditions of Sale*, after completing all required paperwork, and after having a clear understanding when you will get paid.

> ✓ Once the merchandise has been sold at Auction and you have been paid, you're done with this option...*Cross it off the list*.

HOME DOWNSIZING TIP: Remember that all Auctioneers are not the same. Try to locate the best Auctioneer to sell your particular merchandise. Referrals by friends and past satisfied customers, and length of time in the business, are usually two positive indicators to look for in an Auctioneer.

conduct your Garage Sale.

8) Garage Sale, Tag Sale or other Retail Venue: Now the better items should be gone. If you have followed the *AVID Home Downsizing System™*, you will have identified the general value of things and by now disposed of them in the most appropriate venue. Assuming that you have done this, I have no problem with Garage Sales. And frankly, a Garage Sale at this point is probably your last chance to obtain any value at all on your remaining merchandise, before having to dump it.

After following the *Garage Sale Home Downsizing Tips* in Chapter 8, you can

> ✓ Once the final Garage Sale is over, once you have sold whatever is left and worth selling, and once you have been paid, you're done with this option...*Cross it off the list*.

HOME DOWNSIZING TIP: Remember that you should not sell anything at a Garage Sale until you have a general idea of what it's worth in today's market.

---

9) Minor Items Donations. After the Garage Sale is over, you will still have certain items of value remaining. Rather than throwing them away, contact a local non-profit organization

and see if they will pick them up...at no charge. Such donations can help those seriously in need, and lead you to the final *Home Downsizing* step.

✓ Once you have donated your final item, and it has been picked up and is gone, you're done with this option...*Cross it off the list*.

HOME DOWNSIZING TIP: There are many Thrift Stores and Non-Profits to choose from. Try to select one whose aims and goals are similar to yours.

10) Cleanout Specialist or Dumpster: The primary difference between these two options is "*Who does it*"? and "*How much will it cost*"?. The final decision in this step doesn't have to be made until you have executed your *Plan of Action*, and everything else is gone. At this point you basically you have three options for disposing of any remaining unsold items.

- If you only have a few items remaining, and if you prefer to handle it yourself, you can probably put the final cleanout items by the curb for a local trash pick-up at little or no expense to you.
- If you have a substantial amount of items remaining, and if you prefer to handle it by yourself, you can order a dumpster, and fill it with what's left.
- If you have a substantial amount of items remaining, and if you prefer not to handle it by yourself, you can hire a Cleanout Specialist to handle it for you.

✓ And once the final cleanout is over, you're done with this option...*Cross it off the list*.

* * * * *

That's it. You're now done with the *Personal Property* portion of the *AVID Home Downsizing System™*. And hopefully you have received fair value on the vast majority of your *Personal Property* assets. And best of all, you are now fully downsized.

If you are staying in your current home for a while, that's it. You're done. There is no need to go any further in this book at this time.

If your current plans include *Moving*, let's take you to the next step: *Packing and Moving*.

Plan of Action Final Checklist

                                        Pending   *Completed*

1) Initial Dump

2) Keeping It

3) Family and Friends

4) Major Item Donations

5) Selling It Privately

6) Selling It On eBay or the Internet

7) Public Auction

8) Garage Sale, Tag Sale, Retail Venue

9) Minor Item Donations

10) Cleanout Specialist or Dumpster

FINAL STEPS

Packing and Moving On

You have now disposed of all of your excess, unwanted and un-need Personal Property. It's gone. In Chapters 20-22 we'll provide you with a wide variety of Tips & Strategies on how to pack your remaining Personal Property, how to select a Moving Company, and how best to complete the move into your new home.

✓ *Proper Packing Techniques: Getting It There Safely*: In Chapter 20 we'll review with you proper techniques for packing a wide variety of merchandise, and how to get it to your next destination safely.

✓ <u>Selecting the Right Moving Company</u>: There are thousands of Moving Companies around the country and they are not all the same. In Chapter 21 we'll review with you what to look for when selecting the right moving company.

✓ *Meet the Cleanout Specialist*: You've kept the best merchandise, or have given it away to family and friends. You've sold what was sellable. What do you do with what's left? Meet the *Cleanout Specialist*. If you're in the 50-75+ age group, I don't have to remind you that your back isn't as strong as it once was. If you are not in a position to handle to final cleanout and cleanup yourself, there is an army of "*younger backs*" willing to do it for you...*for a price*. In Chapter 22 we'll explain to you how the *Cleanout Specialist* works.

Chapter 20

Getting It There Safely: The Art of Packing

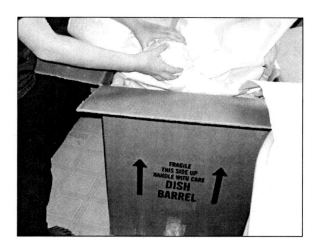

Most people do not enjoy packing, particularly if it's a large packing job. It's time consuming, your hands will get dirty, and your floor will become a mess.

However, no one wants to have their *Personal Property* damaged due to poor packing either. It is critical to the success of your move that the contents of your home be packed and moved correctly, and protected while in transit. Proper packing supplies and packing techniques will reduce the chances that your *Personal Property* will be damaged during your move.

The safest and easiest way to pack is to hire professional packers to do your packing for you. If you do not have the ability or the time to pack, and if you are able to hire a professional packing service, do it.

However it is extremely important that the packing be completed in advance of, and not on moving day. You should understand that moving men are not necessarily professional packers, and professional packers are not necessarily moving men. If you fail to pack ahead of time, you may end up watching your moving men standing around while you finish the packing. On moving day the last thing you want is your moving men on a break, billing you by the hour, waiting for you to finish packing.

If your budget does not allow you to hire a packing service, doing your own packing can save you a considerable amount of money. If you choose to personally pack the contents of your home you will need to know what materials to use, and how to safely pack each item to prevent damage.

When packing for your move, a little common sense goes a long way. Visualize a stack of fine china in a box on the bed of a bouncing truck. No matter how well the sides are padded, a firm up-and-down jolt could crack the entire stack. On the other hand, dishes packed on edge, and surrounded by bubble wrap in a solid moving box, have a better chance of surviving the trip unharmed.

This chapter will contain useful tips and strategies on what to pack, what not to pack, and how to pack different items. Subsections in this chapter include:
- *Packing Supplies and Tools Needed*
- *Plan Before You Pack Your First Box*
- *Packing 101: General Packing Tips*
- *Advanced Packing 201: Thinking Ahead*
- *How to Pack Specific Items*
- *If You Are Loading Your Own Truck*

* * * * * * * *

Packing Supplies and Tools Needed

Having the right tools on hand will make your packing job significantly easier and will help to eliminate unnecessary breakage. In the long run it pays to purchase the right packing materials. Sturdy boxes, packing tape, bubble wrap, and packing peanuts can be purchased from moving companies, rental truck companies, or office supply stores. When you calculate the up-front cost of better packing materials against the potential loss due to breakage, the cost doesn't seem quite as significant.

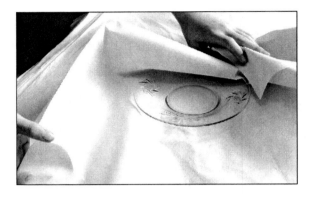

- *Dedicated Work Area or Tables*: Select a work area of sufficient space to handle various size boxes and all of the packing you will have to do. A strong table with a protective cover will save you time and frustration during the packing process. The last thing you want is a table with weak legs crashing to the floor with a box of glass. We suggest you not use your good dining room table for obvious reasons. Consider using a newer light weight, heavy duty plastic top table. Keep your marking pens, tape and scissors conveniently nearby. Spread a neatly stacked, generous amount of packing paper flat on your table for easy access and packing.

- *Cardboard Boxes*: Use small, medium, and large boxes as needed. Although free liquor store boxes may work for a small move, they will prove inadequate for a larger move. The biggest problem with these boxes is that they are flimsier and do not stack well. When you are trying to fill a truck, whether your rental truck or the mover's truck, you need to stack boxes high in order to conserve space. And stacking flimsy liquor store boxes too high will tend to crush the boxes on the bottom, thereby causing more damage and breakage than you would like.

- These additional materials that can be purchased from most moving companies:
  - o 1.5 Cu. Ft. Cartons - These are small cartons for heavy items such as books, tools and records.
  - o 3.1 Cu. Ft. Cartons - These are medium utility cartons and are often used for lighter items such as pots and pans, toys, etc.
  - o Mirror Carton - Various sizes of telescoping cartons will fit almost any picture, mirror, or glass that may have to be moved.
  - o Mattress Covers - These are available in king, queen, double, single (twin), and crib sizes.
  - o Dish Box or China Barrel - These are heavy-duty boxes or barrels used for dishes, china, crystal, glassware, and other fragile items.
  - o Wardrobe Carton: These are portable closets that keep clothes hanging neatly.

- *Newspaper or Blank Newsprint*: Have an ample supply of plain newsprint and newspaper. Newspaper that you may have saved is free, but it will make your hands filthy and could cause stains to certain items such as linens, clothing, etc. You can purchase blank newsprint, cut to ideal packing size, from your moving company. Or, in certain areas you can get free *"end rolls"* from your local newspaper publisher. (*End Rolls* are newsprint without ink). Some newspapers give them away for free, others charge a token amount.

- *Packing Tape with a Tape Dispenser*. Use 1.5"-2.0" heavy duty packing tape for tightly sealing your boxes. Avoid using duct tape, masking tape, or scotch tape as they are not strong enough for the job.

- *Cardboard For Use As Dividing Spacers*: This is to prevent damage from items rubbing against each other.

- *Styrofoam Peanuts, Pellets or Popcorn*: Although more expensive, this makes excellent packing material and provides superior padding and protection.

- *Bubble Wrap*: This can be useful when wrapping certain types of glassware, china, figurines, knick-knacks, etc.

- *Tissue and Kraft Paper*: This can also be useful when wrapping certain types of glassware, figurines, knick-knacks, etc.

- *Pre-Printed Computer Labels, Box Stickers, or Magic Markers*: These will be helpful in identifying what's in the box if you need to locate something after packing it, or in identifying where the box will go in your new home.

- *Utility Knife and Scissors*: You may need these for cutting cardboard, boxes, tape, or many other uses.

- *Larger Heavy-Duty Plastic Trash Bags*: These may be handy for packing clothing, coats, linens, shower curtains, or other such soft and pliable items.

- *Smaller Clear Plastic Bags*: These can be useful for securing nuts, bolts, screws, and other parts when disassembling things like toys, swing sets, beds, etc.

- *Pad of Paper or Notebook and Pens*: For making any notes needed to jog your memory later.

- *Lots of Patience.*

* * * * * * * * * *

Plan Before You Pack Your First Box

Once you have your packing supplies in order, create a *Packing Plan* before you pack your first box.

- *Proper Packing Technique Pays Off*: Proper packing technique, and using the right materials, will mean an easier move with fewer damaged pieces.

- *Set Up Your Packing Area First*. Before packing your first box, set up your tables and packing area. Keep everything together in an easily findable area. Once you start packing, with boxes, papers, and supplies all around the room, it becomes very easy to lose things which can cost you valuable packing time while you look for the lost tool that you need.

- *Plan To Pack One Room At A Time*. This will make unpacking that much easier because it will help to keep similar items together. It will also help you to gauge how well your packing is progressing. It's best not to mix items from different rooms in one box.

- *Pack Several Boxes Each Day*: If time is of the essence, begin by packing several boxes each day, several weeks prior to your move, and watch how easy the packing becomes. Of course be certain that the items you pack won't be needed before your move. By pacing yourself, you'll be more organized and the job won't be so overwhelming.

- *Develop You Own Labels Or Identification System*: Label each box with a description of its contents and its destination (e.g., kitchen, bathroom). Be as specific as you can. This will help if you need to locate something after it has been packed. Write a general description of the box contents and indicate either which room it came from, or better yet, which room it will go to in your new home. Use different colored dot stickers for each room.

- *If Moving In The Summer*: Recognize that the inside of a trailer gets very warm, especially in the summer. Consider moving temperature-sensitive items either yourself, or by other means.

- *Seasonal Items:* Pack seasonal or rarely used items that you know will not be needed before the move first.

- *Pack Similar Items Together*: Pack fragile items together, kitchen items together, etc.

- *Pack By Weight:* Pack heavy items with heavy items, and light items with light items.

- *Plan Box Weight*: Plan your packing so that no box weighs more than 50 pounds, if at all possible.

- *Box-To-Weight Rule of Thumb*: A general rule of thumb on box size is...the heavier the item, the smaller the box.

- *Ask Your Mover For Packing Tips*: If you are packing yourself, you can ask your mover to provide you with suggestions on proper selection of packing materials & containers, and other related packing tips.

Packing 101: General Packing Tips

- *Use Appropriate Bottom Padding*: Start with a padded layer of crushed paper on the bottom of the box for extra cushioning. Supplement your careful packing with generous amounts of crumpled paper, blankets and pillows; or anything else that can serve as a buffer between potentially breakable objects.

- *Keep Sets Together*: Keep sets and similar items in the same box.

- *Free Liquor Store Boxes*: Many liquor stores give their empty boxes away for free. Divided boxes designed to hold 750ml and 1.5 ml bottles can be good for packing certain types of china, glass, cups, vases, etc. But don't over-pack them as they can be quite flimsy. Don't use compartmentalized liquor boxes unless the compartments are sturdy. Put a layer of packing material on the bottom first. Glasses and cups should still be wrapped in bubble wrap or wrapping paper. And stack these boxes on top, not on the bottom of other boxes.

- *Monitor the Packing*: If the moving company or anyone else is packing your household goods, monitor the wrapping and packing of your items. Make sure everything is wrapped individually and adequately.

- *Beware of Packing Hazardous Materials*: Hazardous materials should not be included in your shipment. Some common household items that cannot be packed include flamables such as paint, varnish & thinners, gasoline, kerosene & oil, bottled gas, aerosol cans, nail polish & remover, ammunition & explosives, corrosives, and cleaning fluids & detergents.

- *Carry Valuables Yourself*: Personally carry irreplaceable photos, financial papers and assets (bank checks, insurance policies, stock certificates, etc.), legal documents (wills, passports. etc.), valuables (jewelry, coin and stamp collections, etc.), and medical and family history records.

- *Make A First-Day List*: Make a list of those items you may need on the last day in your old house, or first day in your new home, and pack these items separately.

- *Mark Boxes For The Moving Men*: Mark all boxes, designating room and box number. Your carton identification log should show the number of boxes packed per room, and the total number of cartons packed. This will help the movers to know where to put each box in your new home.

- *Use Extra Filler Material*: Be certain to have plenty of "*filler*" material such as crushed newspaper or styrofoam peanuts available. When in doubt, use more rather than less.

- *Secure Box Bottoms*: Take extra care to make sure the bottoms of all cartons are secured and will hold the weight of the contents. Re-tape where appropriate.

141

- *Protect Fragile Items*: Generously add at least two inches of crumpled paper cushion between fragile items, and on all sides of the box.

- *Layered Packing*: As you pack each layer of a box, use crumpled packing paper to assure a snug fit wherever there's a gap. All boxes that contain "*fragile*" items should be so marked.

- *Pack It Right*: Moving Companies have the right to inspect packed-by-owner boxes to insure packing is adequate to protect your goods during transit. If, in the mover's judgment a container is packed improperly, the carrier may ask the customer to re-pack it; or, the carrier representative may choose to re-pack the container and charge you for the service. If any packed-by-owner container is damaged in transit, the mover's liability may be affected.

HOME DOWNSIZING TIP: Family and friends can be very helpful in the packing process. But if they are not careful packers, their "*Free*" help can cost you considerable money in broken or damaged merchandise.

Advanced Packing 201: Thinking Ahead

- *Be Careful Of Where You Place Tape*: Don't apply tape directly to polished or painted wood finishes. Removing the tape could ruin the surface.

- *Double Box Where Appropriate*: Double-box fragile items and add plenty of cushioning.

- *Load Important Boxes Last*: When everything is packed and ready to load, make sure the items you need most are loaded last.

- *Plan Multiple Delivery Points*: If your move includes multiple delivery points, clearly identify which boxes are to be delivered to which location. Color coding works well here.

- *Special Packing*: Double box your especially fragile or valuable items, such as your best Hummel Figurines, in bubble wrap, then inside a coffee can, and then inside a well-padded box.

- *Special Packing for Miniature Items*. To prevent small items from being lost or mistakenly thrown out with the packing paper, wrap miniature knick-knacks and other small items in brightly-colored paper before placing them in the box.

- *Safe Un-Packing Techniques*. Unpack fragile items and breakables over some packing material or over the box you're taking them out of in case you happen to drop the item as you unpack it.

How to Pack Specific Items

The section provides specific ideas on how to pack a wide variety of items. It is not 100% complete, but should serve to give you a general idea on how to pack most of the items in your household.

Appliances and Utensils
- Be sure to defrost, clean and dry all applicable appliances before the movers arrive.
- Have an authorized serviceman prepare all large appliances (refrigerator, stove, freezer, washer, dryer, etc.) for moving.
- Wrap and place small appliances and utensils in sturdy cartons with the heavier items on the bottom.

Artwork, Pictures & Prints
- For lower value pictures, prints, and frames, place them in the box back-to-back, and front-to-front to avoid eye screw damage to the glass and frames. Use crumpled newspaper between the frames to prevent movement in the box.
- For more fragile pictures like oil-on-canvas, wrap carefully in a quilted moving blanket and/or store carefully in an appropriately-sized picture box.
- For higher value pictures and prints, wrap individually and pack safely. Double box and transport separately, if necessary.

Barbeque Grills and Propane Tanks
- Wrap grates and briquettes separately in newspaper, or place all briquettes into a grocery bag, and place parts in a separate bag or container.
- Pad the carton with paper to reduce movement of contents.
- Propane tanks will not be accepted even if they have been purged by an authorized gas grill distributor. Plan to properly dispose of the old tank prior to your move, and purchase a new one when you arrive at your new home, or transport it yourself.

Books
- Use book cartons since they are intentionally smaller to prevent over-packing.
- Wrap each better book, then lay them flat, alternating the spine and open side from book to book.
- Books are deceptively heavy so don't over-pack book boxes.
- Consider selling or donating books that you will never use again. Why pack and pay to move something that you will probably never read again?

Canned Goods and Other Non-Frozen Foods
- Try to use up as much of these as possible prior to your move date. Why pay to move a can of beans?
- Pack upright in an appropriately-sized box with no more than 24-30 cans per carton. Canned food can be quite heavy.

- Wrap glass containers and boxed foods individually and pack in small cartons. These items should also be packed in smaller boxes. Don't over-pack.

Cars and Motorcycles
- Cars and motorcycles shipped on the moving van should be drained of fuel.
- Batteries should be disconnected.
- Antifreeze should be sufficient to protect against severe cold in winter.

Chandeliers
- Valuable and/or delicate chandeliers can be fully protected in special double-or triple-walled chandelier cartons, complete with hanging bar.
- Oversize chandeliers may require custom built wooden crates.
- Let your mover pack these.

Chest of Drawers
- Don't overload. Overloaded drawers can cause damage to the bureau during the move.
- Remove valuables and any items that might break or leak.

China & Dishes
- Carefully wrap each piece in newspaper or preferably blank newsprint. You don't want ink to transfer and permanently stain your porcelain or china.
- After wrapping each piece put 2-3 plates together and wrap them again. Tape together where appropriate. Place the plates on their edge in the box.
- Nest 3-4 wrapped bowls at a time and wrap them again.
- Add newspaper cushioning between each set.
- Put larger pieces on the bottom of the box and build up to the lighter weight dishes.
- Cushion all sides with at least two inches of crumpled newspaper.

Clocks
- Remove or secure the pendulum in larger clocks.
- Tall case and other valuable clocks should be prepared for moving by expert servicemen.

Clothing
- Use wardrobe cartons for packing clothing on hangers in order to reduce wrinkles and to make moving your clothing easier.
- With wardrobe boxes all you do is remove the clothing from your closet and hang it in the wardrobe box. Not only is it easier and time efficient, your clothes will arrive ready-to-wear and will neatly hang in your new closet.
- Clothing in chests of drawers can be left in the drawers or packed in boxes at your discretion.

Collectibles
- Whenever possible pack collectibles in their original boxes.
- Otherwise wrap each item with multiple layers of paper and bubble wrap.
- The first layer should be blank newsprint to prevent staining.
- Depending upon rarity and value, consider double and triple boxing.

Computers & Electronics

- Unplug prior to packing in enough time to allow them to cool down before the move.
- Secure or remove any moveable parts, cords, etc.
- Where possible pack in the original box.
- Use bubble wrap or other special cushioning material where appropriate.
- If moving in winter weather don't plug in electronics until they have reached room temperature.
- Computers and printers will require special care. Wires and cables must be disconnected and special care should be taken to protect the hard drive.
- Monitors and hardware should be wrapped in a manner similar to other home electronics.
- Back-up all important files prior to the move...just in case your hard drive is damaged.

Flammables and Combustibles

- Flammable liquids and aerosol cans must not be packed. Changes in temperature and pressure can cause them to leak or even explode.
- If you pack these items and they cause damage, you, not your mover, will be held liable.
- Take any state and local laws into consideration during your move.

Glassware, Teacups and Stemware

- Use heavy-duty boxes or dish barrel cartons. Wrap each glass or teacup in a piece of bubble wrap and tape it.
- Otherwise use boxes with special dividers. Liquor store boxes can work well for this task. But be wary of overloading.
- Put a layer of peanuts or crushed newsprint on the bottom of the box.
- Stuff the goblet with a wad of paper and then wrap the entire piece in multiple layers of crumpled paper.
- Lay glass or stemware on the corner of packing paper and roll it with two full rotations, then pull sides of packing paper up and over glass/stemware and continue rolling to the far corner. Corrugated paper rolls may be used for added protection
- Place wrapped cups or glasses on top, upright as if you were placing them on the table.
- Place a layer of cardboard and another layer of packing material on top and the sides.
- Keep layering in wrapped cups and packing material until you've reached the top. Put a final layer of packing material on top, tape the box closed, and mark it "*Fragile - Crystal/China*".
- Stemware should be placed toward the top of your box. Heavier items such as dishware or pitchers should be placed toward the bottom of the box. Very delicate glassware and stemware should be placed in a vertical position, lips down, not on their sides.

Heavy or Hard-to-Move Items

- Recognize that certain items, due to high value or fragility, may need special care and packing. Fine Antiques, expensive Art, slate pool tables, pianos, marble top tables, bars, and tall case clocks come to mind. Be certain to go over this with your mover in advance of moving day.

Lamps
- Remove the shade, globe and light bulb.
- Wrap the globe and the lamp base separately in unprinted newsprint or newspaper.
- Place in the box base side down.
- Generously surround with newspaper.
- Wrap the shades separately.
- They can then be nested and wrapped again before being placed in the box.
- As always, cushion all sides of the box with at least two inches of paper.

Linens & Pillows
- You can use day-to-day linens and pillows as cushioning for delicate items as long as they will not become soiled or damaged during the move.
- For better and more decorative pillows use a larger box. Wardrobe boxes can be effectively used to move lighter-weight pillows, linens, comforters, blankets and pillows together.
- Or place these items at the bottom of the clothing wardrobe boxes.
- Linens can also be placed in clean boxes or in bureau drawers.

Medicines
- Seal caps with masking tape.
- Wrap and pack upright in small cartons.
- Some prescription drugs, such as insulin, lose their potency if exposed to heat.
- Carry any important medications with you.

Microwave Ovens
- Remove all loose articles inside the oven, such as cookware, glass shelves, and carousels.
- Wrap loose articles and place in a separate container.
- Tape the door shut with an "X"-pattern over the door and glass to protect the glass.
- Transport in the original box if available.

Mirrors and Glass Tabletops
- Use paper generously to wrap mirrors, pictures and glass.
- Use telescoping boxes where appropriate.
- Always stand glass and mirrors on their edge.

Phonographs and Compact Disc Players
- Use original cartons and packing materials when available.
- Secure the changer and tone arm of phonograph.
- Tighten down the screws that are often located on the top of the turntable to stabilize it.
- Wrap the dust cover in soft tissue or pad it with old linen to protect against surface scratches.
- Wrap the unit with an old blanket and place it upright in carton.
- Refer to your owner's manual where appropriate.

Plates and Bowls
- Use heavy-duty boxes or dish barrel cartons and stand all plates on edge in the containers.

- Place crushed newsprint or peanuts in the bottom of a box and put layers of plates or bowls on top. Then fill in the top and sides with peanuts or newsprint.
- Layer bubble wrap in between, leaving space at the top of the box to fill in with crushed newsprint.
- Tape the box closed and mark it "*Fragile - China.*"

Records, Tapes and CDs
- Layer the bottom of a small carton with shredded or crushed paper.
- Records without sleeves should be wrapped with tissue paper or plastic wrap to prevent scratching.
- Pack records and CDs on edge (do not lay flat).
- Brace at both ends using a hardback book or layer pieces of cardboard to provide a snug fit.
- Compact Disks should be in their protective cases.
- If not, wrap individual tapes in paper.
- Place either vertically or horizontally on layers of shredded or crushed paper. Fill in with paper as needed.

Rugs
- Better hand-knotted Oriental Rugs should be folded, not rolled.
- Most other rugs can be rolled with the bottom facing out, and then secured with heavy-duty plastic tape.

Shoes
- Clean your shoes first, and then wrap each shoe separately.
- After wrapping each shoe, wrap each pair together and place in the original shoebox where possible.
- Otherwise wrap by the pair and keep shoes within the same larger box.

Silverware, Flatware and Kitchenware
- Wrap each piece in cloth or low sulphur content paper to prevent tarnishing.
- Use an old blanket or moving pad as a wrap to avoid scratching the silverware box or chest.
- Any sharp edged item should be wrapped carefully to prevent injury to you or the movers.
- Pack silver together and wrap securely so it does not shift and scratch.
- Be especially careful with Sterling Silver due to its premium value in today's market.
- Wrap kitchen utensils individually where appropriate and cushion.

Tools and Lawn Equipment
- Drain oil and fuel from power tools such as mowers, blowers, trimmers, and chain saws.
- Never ship flammable liquids under any circumstances.
- Pack hand tools in small, strong cartons. Wrap separately if valuable.

Video Tapes
- Place videos on edge in a small carton.
- When stacking, layer with paper in between to protect from scratching.
- Fill in around edges with crumpled paper to secure.

Waterbed Mattresses
- Drain all water from the waterbed and carefully fold the mattress.
- Consult your owner's manual for special instructions concerning the care and transportation of your mattress.

* * * * * * * * * *

If your Are Loading Your Own Truck

If you prefer to move yourself, you can rent a truck, van, or trailer from a variety of rental companies. Rental moving trucks can range from 10'-26', and trailers can vary in size from 4'x8' – 6'-12' and larger.

There are many national truck rental companies with most having truck rental centers throughout the country. Web sites for just a few of them include:
- www.uhaul.com
- www.BudgetTruck.com
- www.ryder.com
- www.PenskeTruckRental.com

Having proper moving supplies can make the self-moving job even easier, and can be rented from your truck rental center. Some of the most commonly rented items include:
- *Quilted Moving Pads*: These will protect your furniture and other items from scratches and other blemishes.
- *Furniture Dolly*: These will help you move larger pieces of furniture, or several boxes at once.
- *Appliance Dolly*: These special dollies are designed to help you move refrigerators or other larger appliances.
- *Specialty Boxes*: These are ideal for packing difficult-to-move things like artwork, mirrors, glass tabletops, etc.

Loading Tips: Loading items properly inside your truck will make the ride smoother and unloading much easier. Here are some basic loading tips.
- *Rent the Proper Size Truck*: Rent too big and you are throwing money away. Rent too small and you will have to make two trips.
- *Load the Heaviest Items First*: The heaviest items should always be loaded first, which will provide added stability when on the road.
- *Use Common Sense*: Common sense is essential when loading the truck. Place the box containing your best china on top of the box of books and not vice versa.

- *Load the Truck in Stages*: Pack the truck 1/4 at a time. Pack it tightly, from the floor to ceiling, before proceeding to the next section. Secure each section with belts or rope attached to the tie-down rings to reduce the chances of a shifting load.
- *Larger Items to the Front*. Position larger items such as china closets, sideboards, chest of drawers, sofas, refrigerators, and other heavy appliances against the front wall of the truck. Then build up with boxes on top of them.
- *Stand Bedding on End*: Position larger, flat items such as tabletops, mattresses, box springs, and mirrors upright against the truck walls and secure them.
- *Protect Bedding and Upholstered Pieces*: Use protective covers on sofas and mattresses.
- *Pictures & Mirrors*: Protect pictures and mirrors by wrapping them with protective pads or use a special mirror carton and store them on end.
- *Chairs, Tables & Lighter Items*: Load chairs, tables, bookcases and other lighter furniture items towards the back of the truck.
- *Stacking Boxes*: Stack smaller, lighter boxes on top of larger, heavier ones.
- *Keep Important Boxes Where You Can See Them*: Load important boxes that you may need towards the rear of the truck where you can see them, just in case you need to access them.
- *Carry Valuables with You*: Keep valuables such as stocks, bonds, cash, securities, etc. with you so they are not lost, damaged or stolen.

Chapter 21

Moving Tips: Dealing with the Moving Man

A good move depends largely on how well prepared you are when the movers arrive. This chapter will focus upon how to select and effectively deal with moving companies. We are not professional movers or moving experts but we have assembled approximately 20 pages of thoughts, questions, tips, strategies, and ideas to help you through the moving phase of your *Home Downsizing* process.

Moving across town can be stressful enough. Moving across a state or across the country can be even more stressful. People rarely describe the experience of moving their entire household as "*fun.*" It totally consumes you for a long time: planning, packing, moving, cleaning. And when you arrive in your new home, you're faced with even more challenges.

Subsections in this chapter include:
- Questions To Ask Yourself Prior To Beginning A Move
- Selecting and Dealing With A Moving Company
- Questions To Ask The Moving Company
- Tips On Selecting The Right Moving Company
- Scheduling A Moving Date
- Pre-Moving Day Tips
- Things To Leave For The New Owner Of Your Home
- Before Moving Into Your New Home
- Preparing Your Family For The Move
- Pets and Plants
- Moving Day Tips
- As You Leave Your Old Home
- Arrival Day At Your New Home

Questions To Ask Yourself Prior To Beginning A Move

Local or Long Distance Move: Will your move be a "*local*" or a "*long distance*" move? Obviously the farther you move, the more expensive and difficult your move will be. There are some key differences between local moves and long distance moves that you should be aware of.
- You will generally be charged per man-hour for local moves (i.e., moves of less than 40 miles), and by volume, weight and/or distance for long distance moves (moves greater than 40 miles).
- On local moves you will normally be charged for point-to-point service, as opposed to when the moving truck and crew arrives at your house.
- Moving costs will be based on the amount of property that must be moved, and the time it takes to move it. Moving time will be further impacted by elevators, flights of

stairs, length of walk, proximity to the house that the moving truck can park, etc., as each of these conditions will impact the time it takes to move you.
- Some movers will include the costs of padding, boxes, and other moving supplies in the cost of the move. Others will add it on.

Who's Doing the Packing? Are you packing yourself, is the moving company packing for you, or is some third party doing the packing? We discussed packing in Chapter 20. If the moving company is also doing your packing, you can sometimes negotiate a better deal on the entire job.

Who's Moving You? Are you moving yourself in a rented truck or van, or will you be hiring a professional moving company to move you?

Will You Need Temporary Storage? Life will be easier if you can move immediately into your new home and settle in. But if your new home isn't quite ready, or if you must be out of your current home faster than you expected, you may need some temporary storage. Many moving companies offer temporary storage but others do not. Ask your mover if they have temporary storage capabilities. If they do, here are some questions you should ask them before moving your items into their temporary storage facility:

- Is the temporary storage facility secure? Who else will have access to your things?
- Is it dry and temperature controlled?
- Can you access it if you need to retrieve something? Is there a cost associated with this?
- Is your property insured while in storage? For how much? Is there additional coverage for fire, flood, etc? How much does this cost?
- If your plans should change, what is the additional cost for extra storage time?
- Is there an added cost for moving your property after additional months in storage?

Self-Storage With Another Company: If your mover doesn't offer temporary storage, or if their rates are prohibitive, you can seek temporary storage elsewhere. Most self-storage facilities require you to bring your property to them so, although their storage rates may be cheaper, the additional labor required for the double handling may make this option cost prohibitive. In addition to the questions above, you should also ask these questions of a self storage company:
- Is there a security deposit?
- Are there any early termination fees? What are the late fees?

- When can you access your storage facility? Some self-storage facilities are closed on Sunday, don't open until 6:00 AM, etc.
- Do you need to insure the goods yourself? Some Homeowners Insurance policies may not cover property that you put in storage.
- How much space do you need?

Portable On Demand Storage (PODS): Another option is on-location self-storage. These companies bring empty mini-storage sheds to your house. When you fill them up, they take them either directly to your new home, or temporarily to their storage facility, depending upon your situation. This is a relatively new concept and it may or may not work in your situation. However, it is definitely worth investigating.

Tips Designed to Save Money on Your Move: Here are a few ideas designed to save money on your move. We'll provide additional moving tips throughout this chapter.
- *If You Don't Need It, Don't Move It*. It will much cheaper to sell or dump something before the move, rather than pay to move it, only to dump it later.
- *Pack Yourself*: Consider packing yourself. This may have moving insurance implications, so check with your mover and your Insurance Agent.
- *Buy Your Moving Supplies On-line*. Moving supplies can often be purchased less expensively when purchased in advance and online.
- *Improvise with Packing Supplies*. Newspaper usually works as well for packing as does inkless paper, and it's free.
- *Borrow Your Moving Tools*. Why buy a tape dispenser that you'll only use once? Borrow one from a friend.
- *Beware of Excessive Packing*. Ask your mover how they'll be packing your items. Some movers packing costs may exceed the value of what they are packing.
- *Do You Really Need Moving Insurance*? Do you really need moving insurance? If you raise the deductible, will it significantly lower the cost of insurance? 400N Tariff moving companies must offer 60 cents of insurance per pound per item as part of the basic package. Is that enough? What is covered by your Homeowner's Insurance?
- *Move Yourself*. This can save you big money if you, along with family and friends, can move you.
- *Anticipate Transitional Moving Costs*. Motel stays, dining out, pet boarding, etc. can all add to your moving expense. Don't forget to anticipate any additional costs that you may incur while in transition.

Selecting and Dealing With a Moving Company

400N Tariff Overview: The *400N Tariff* is a rules and regulations document that is designed to protect the consumer. Among other things, it provides that:
- Movers must give written estimates.
- Movers may give binding estimates.

- Non-binding estimates are not always accurate, and actual charges may exceed the estimate. However 400N Tariff movers will often offer "*not to exceed*" weight-based estimates based on your reported inventory.
- You may request from your mover the availability of guaranteed pickup and delivery dates.
- You have the right to be present each time your shipment is weighed.
- You may request a re-weigh of your shipment.
- Movers must offer a dispute settlement program as an alternative means of settling loss or damage claims. The details vary by mover, but don't forget to ask about this. You may also request complaint information about movers from the *Federal Motor Carrier Safety Administration* under the *Freedom of Information Act*. You will probably be charged a fee to obtain this information.
- You should seek estimates from at least three different moving companies. Do not disclose information to the different movers about their competitors quote, as it may affect their estimates.
- Movers must offer a minimum level of insurance on all property (currently 60 cents per pound per item).

Dealing with the Moving Company
- *Book a Moving Date Early*: Contact the moving company early and get a moving estimate long before your anticipated moving date. You might be able to save money by booking early.
- *Disclose All Large Items*: Show the moving agent everything that is going to be moved. Any items you fail to disclose or that are added later to the shipment will increase the cost, even if you have been given a binding estimate.
- *Read the Paperwork Carefully*: Read all related paperwork to make certain that you fully understand the extent of the carrier's liability and your responsibility. If you have any doubts, have an attorney or advisor read it for you.
- *Don't Sign Until You Are 100% Certain*: Sign the moving contract only after you are sure you have a clear understanding of each point. If you have any questions, ask your agent to explain, before you sign anything.
- *Notify Your Mover of Any Last Minute Changes*: You have the right to make last minute changes, and you probably will. However, remember to notify your agent if you add or subtract items from your planned move, or if there are any changes in dates. Be sure to supply your agent with a destination address and phone numbers where you can be reached.
- *Confirm Any Extra Stops*: Confirm any extra stops required to pick up or deliver goods to a location other than the main pickup or delivery points.

Moving Company Pre-Move Responsibilities. Prior to moving day, the moving company has various tasks that it will be responsible for.
- *Pre-Move Survey or Questionnaire*. Prior to your moving day, your mover will probably contact you for a Pre-Move survey. This gives them an idea of how much packing may be involved, how many men and trucks must be committed to your job, and how long they estimate the job will take.
- *Special Handling Items*: They will determine whether you have any items that may require special handling, such as pianos, chandeliers, larger-than-normal furniture, etc.
- *Packing*: If they are handling your packing, the mover must:
  - Use new, clean packing materials for linen, clothing and bedding.

o Pack mirrors, pictures, and glass tabletops in specially designed cartons.
o Properly roll and protect rugs and rug pads.
o Mark each carton to show its general contents.

On Moving Day The Moving Company Should:
- *Arrive Promptly*.
- *Protect Appliances Against Damage*: Appliances must be protected against damage while in transit. This mean the mover will secure any moving parts that, if allowed to move in transit, could damage the appliance.
- *Protect Against Breakage & Scratches*: They should wrap and protect all finished surfaces from marring or scratching.
- *Secure Hardware from Disassembled Items*: In preparation for shipment, nuts, bolts, screws, small hardware, and other fasteners removed by the mover will be placed in a box or bag and securely stored where they will not be lost.
- *Inventory*: They will usually prepare an accurate and legible inventory.
- *Remove Excess Packing Material*: The mover must remove all excess packing material from your residence at the end of the move.

Your Role On Moving Day Is To Insure:
- Each carton and unboxed item has an inventory tag and appears on the inventory sheet.
- Carefully read the inventory prepared by the mover before you sign it. Make sure all boxes and loose items are listed. Make sure descriptions of major items are completed and accurate.
- Walk through your house to insure all items were placed on the truck by the mover before you leave.
- Keep your moving representative's office and cell numbers handy so you can quickly call if the need arises.

Questions To Ask The Moving Company?

Moving can be daunting, but there are laws that protect you. Although we're not in the business of giving legal advice, we recommend that you stick with an 400N Tariff company. Here are some questions to ask:

- *How Do You Charge For Moving Services*? Local moves are typically charged by the hour. Long distance moves are typically charged by weight and mileage, although other companies charge by volume. Ask your mover how you will be charged.
- *Can You Guarantee That Your Estimates Won't Be Exceeded*? Most moving estimates are generally quite accurate...as long as there are no hidden surprises on your part. If you have selected the right moving company, they will be moving professionals and not looking to cheat you. If you communicate clearly with your mover, ask the right questions, and don't give them any surprises, you probably won't be surprised either.

- *Can You Do An In-House Estimate*? Most moving companies will do an in-home estimate, which will be much more accurate than an over-the-phone, on-line, or off-the-cuff estimate.
- *Are You A Broker Or The Actual Mover*? Many movers that you find online are brokers who coordinate local movers, cross-country shippers, packers, insurance, etc. Although you won't be dealing with the moving company directly, brokers have direct contact with the moving companies.
- *Do You Offer Temporary Storage If I Need It*? How much does it cost? What if I need it longer? Is there an additional cost if you need to access your items while they are in temporary storage? Make sure you understand the costs for additional months and any hidden costs.
- *Are All Parties, Including the Packers and Movers Fully Insured and Bonded*? You don't want a mover who is injured on the job blaming or suing you.
- *What Payment Methods Are Accepted*? While some moving companies accept credit card payment for the full cost of the move, others do not. Ask first.
- *What Is Your Refund policy*? What if you decide not to move? Or if you locate a significantly less expensive mover? Many moving companies have very flexible refund policies, e.g. fully refundable if you cancel within a week or two. Ask about your mover's refund policy,
- *What If Their Moving Estimate Is Incorrect*? Your best defense here is to ask a lot of questions: Make sure you fully understand what the estimate is based on (weight, volume, miles) and how the estimate will be verified and finalized. Good communications and targeted questions should help to avoid this.

Tips on Selecting the Right Moving Company

- *Get Multiple Moving Quotes*: Shop around to find the best mover. Online quotes are generally fast and simple but should always be followed up with a phone conversation so you can ask about hidden costs.
- *Check the BBB*: Check the Better Business Bureau for reputable movers.
- *Book Early to Save*: The moving business is a competitive industry and you can often find deep

discounts if you book early. However, those discounts disappear if you wait and don't book until the last minute.
- *Are the Movers Employees or Temporary Workers*? Generally full-time employees will be gentler on your items than temporary workers. It doesn't hurt to ask.
- *Beware of Unusually Low Estimates*: Be suspicious of any moving estimate that is significantly lower than all the others. Is it a true bargain? Or are there many hidden charges? Ask the right questions.
- *Complicated Moves*: Make sure that the moving company knows in advance if they will have to contend with flights of stairs, elevators, long walks, etc, as this will impact the required moving time.

- *Confirm What Your Insurance Covers*: Call your Insurance Agent to determine what, if any, moving damage will be covered by your Homeowners Insurance coverage. Movers only cover what they pack, and they often only insure it "*by the pound*".
- *Watch For Excessive Mover Padding*: Long-distance moves are usually billed according to weight so beware of movers that use excessive padding to add weight.
- *Confirm Building Restrictions Ahead of Time*: Check with your condo or co-op building manager about restrictions on using the elevator or particular exits on particular days. Verify these restrictions before you sign the moving contract.
- *Beware of Shuttle Moves*: Movers prefer to load your items directly onto their truck without double handling. If they can't get that truck within a few hundred feet of your front door, expect to incur extra costs. In some instances they'll have to use a separate "*shuttle*" vehicle to move your property from your house to the outlying truck. If trees, debris, or other natural obstacles prevent the truck from getting close to your house, the double handling required will cost you money.

Scheduling a Moving Date

- *Be Flexible When Selecting a Moving Date*: Try not to schedule your moving date on the closing date of your residence, on the day you must vacate an apartment, terminate a lease, or the day a cleaning crew is to start cleaning your home. Scheduling a move on these days leaves no room to adjust to unforeseen weather or other problems.
- *Don't Shut Off Utilities Too Early*: It's a good idea to leave your phone and other utilities connected until all property has been moved.
- *Don't Wait Until The End Of The Month*: Limited capabilities during peak moving season means that not everyone can move on the last day of the month. The moving industry suggests that, when possible, a two-day pickup date should be scheduled which provides some flexibility in the event something goes wrong. Moving early in the month can save you money.
- *Weekday Moves Can Save You Money*: Most people prefer to move on weekends. If you can move Tuesday-Thursday, it could save you money.
- *Weekday Moves Offer Certain Conveniences*: If you move on a weekday, banks, utilities and government offices are open which will enable you to complete certain business transactions early.
- *Beware of Inclement Weather*: You cannot control the weather, so plan for the worst giving yourself some flexibility.

Pre-Moving Day Tips

Whom To Notify of Your Move
- Give your forwarding address to the Post Office at least several weeks prior to your move date. An online Change of Address form is available on the United States Postal Service Web Site (www.usps.com).
- Notify your credit card companies, magazine subscriptions, and banks of your change of address, again at least several weeks prior to your move date.
- Mail your new address to friends, relatives, and business colleagues who need to know that you have moved. Or better yet, e-mail them and save yourself the postage.
- Cancel the newspaper(s).

- Order preprinted address labels with your new address as soon as you know it. It makes the change-of-address process much easier. Or better yet, print them out on your computer to save money.
- Be certain that your residence is clean and organized for moving day. All dirty laundry and dishes must be cleaned prior to packing.
- Be certain your home is free from any bug infestation. Movers can refuse to pack and pickup your items if your household goods and home are not clean and organized.
- Dispose of worn out and un-necessary items before the move in order to avoid paying for un-necessary packing, moving, and/or storage expenses.
- Use a video camera or take close-up pictures to record the condition of your furniture and to show what your expensive and valuable items looked like prior to the move. You may need to get them appraised prior to your move.
- Obtain a written appraisal of antique or other especially valuable items to verify value.
- Avoid waxing or oiling wooden Antiques or fine wood furniture before moving because some products might soften the wood or make it sticky, thereby making it vulnerable to imprinting or sticking from furniture pads.
- Do not clean your upholstered furniture before moving. Moisture could cause mold if the furniture must be placed in storage.
- Donate unwanted clothing or household goods to charitable organizations. Obtain receipts showing the items' approximate value for possible tax deductions.
- Begin to use up supplies of canned goods, frozen foods and other household items. Buy only what will be used before moving.
- Have rugs and draperies cleaned. Leave both wrapped when they are returned from the cleaners.
- To save time, rent a carpet shampooer at the same time you rent your truck.
- Mark each box with its contents and destination room. That way, you will know where each box belongs at your new home.

Utilities
- Arrange to have your utilities disconnected at your old home but where possible, keep utilities in service through moving day.
- Arrange to have your utilities connected at your new house prior to moving in.
- If you're moving locally, leave the power and water on at your old address a few extra days so you can go back and clean up after your move.
- Keep a log to check utility service-transfer dates.

Personally Take These Items With You When You Move
- Stocks, bonds, jewelry, coins, coin collections, passports, birth certificates, airline tickets, and items of great sentimental value such as photo albums. Pack them in your suitcases and hand carry them, as well as your purchase receipts, pictures, personal property videotape, appraisals, and any other important papers.
- Pack a personal suitcase that you take with you that includes several days of clothing, toiletries, ATM or Credit Cards, Cash, Check Books, Travelers Checks, and any other items that you may need, in the event that something happens to the moving truck for a day or two.

Don't Forget To Do These Things
- Empty your Safe Deposit Box.

- Collect all items that are being cleaned, stored or repaired (clothing, furs, shoes, watches, etc.).
- Empty your locker at the club, bowling alley or gym.
- Return library books and anything borrowed from friends or neighbors.
- Collect things you may have loaned to others.

Things to Leave For the New Owner of Your Home

- Extra set(s) of house keys.
- Garage door opener(s).
- Any applicable codes to Security Systems, etc.
- Owner's Manuals for any items left in the house (refrigerator, freezer, etc)
- Guarantee or Warranty Information for the above.
- Contact information for local services, e.g., pizza delivery, dry cleaners, Chinese restaurant, lawn maintenance, etc.

Before Moving Into Your New Home?

Where possible you should try to complete certain major projects in your new home, if at all possible, prior to your move. Choose the projects that are the most pressing.
- *Painting*: It's always easier to paint an empty room. There will be no need to move furniture, take down draperies, clear out the closets, or take every picture or mirror off the walls. If at all possible, paint before you move into your new home. All of the related painting tasks such as patching, priming, trim work, base coats and final coats can be significantly easier if you can paint in an empty room.
- *Installing New Carpet*: If you've bought a home that needs to be re-carpeted, it would be significantly easier to replace that carpet before you move in. If your budget won't allow re-carpeting the entire house, just do one floor or room.
- *New Flooring*: Replacing old flooring is a major project, and it's even harder when the room is full of furniture. If time permits, this would be another special project to complete prior to moving in.

Preparing Your Family for the Move

If you are moving out of the area, consider these possibilities:
- Take the family for a farewell visit to some of the local places that hold pleasant memories.
- Have a going-away party for the children and their friends.
- Have some fun for yourself...an open house or an informal dinner or barbecue. Keep it simple and make it fun.
- Make family travel plans. Reserve hotel rooms and airline tickets as needed.
- If driving, have your car serviced for the trip (check tires, brakes and windshield wipers, fluids, belts, etc.)

Plants and Pets

- *Plants*: Decide what to do with house plants. Many movers will not move plants because they may suffer from lack of water and light as well as probable temperature changes while in the van.
- *Plants*: Give plants to friends or relatives instead of moving them.
- *Plants*: Donate plants to a hospital or other organization instead of moving them.
- *Plants*: Sell plants in your garage sale.
- *Plants*: Some states permit the entry of all house plants; others do not. Check this before moving day.

- *Pets*: Many states require health certificates and rabies inoculations. Check it out before moving day.
- *Pets.* Arrange for transportation of pets. Take them in the car or send via air.
- *Pets*: Consider boarding pets either at your new destination or at a kennel near your present home until you are settled in the new city.

Moving Day Tips

- Point out to the packers any extra-fragile items needing special attention.
- Mark any items you do not want packed or moved.
- Mark the cartons you will want first when the van arrives at your final destination.
- Check closets, cabinets, and storage lockers for any articles overlooked.
- Be on hand when the service representative arrives to prepare your appliances for shipment.
- It is your responsibility to see that all mechanical and electrical equipment is properly serviced for shipping prior to the arrival of the moving van at your expense.
- It is your responsibility to see that all of your goods are loaded, so remain on the premises until loading is complete. After making a final tour of the house, check and sign the inventory list. Get your copy from the mover and keep it.
- Approve and sign the Bill of Lading/Freight Bill. It states the terms and conditions under which your goods are moved and is also your receipt for the shipment. Be sure to complete and sign the declared valuation statement.
- Complete and sign the High-Value Inventory form, whether or not items of extraordinary value are included in the shipment. You may also need to sign and date the "*Extraordinary (Unusual) Value Article Declaration*" box on the Bill of Lading, if applicable to your shipment.
- Make sure the mover knows the exact destination address. Be sure to let the van operator know how you can be reached, including cell phone numbers, pending the arrival of your household goods.
- Get up early and be ready for the movers.
- Get your pets under control before the movers arrive. Perhaps letting them stay with a neighbor is an even better idea.
- In the event of snow or sleet, clear your walkways of snow and ice before the movers arrive. If the movers arrive before this job is done, you will be incurring billable moving hours while you get this job done. Don't expect the movers to do it for you.

As You Leave Your Old Home

- Leave your phone connected throughout moving day. After the van leaves and you finish last-minute calls, be sure to pack the phone in one of your suitcases.
- Is the water, furnace and air conditioner shut off?
- Are the light switches turned off?
- Are all utilities disconnected, or arranged for disconnection?
- Are the windows shut and locked?
- Have you left old house keys and other items for the new owners?
- Have you left anything else of value?

Arrival Day at Your New Home

- *Be On Hand To Accept Delivery*. If you cannot be there personally, be sure you authorize an adult to be your representative to accept delivery and pay the charges for you.
- *Be On Time*: On the day of delivery, the mover will attempt to contact you by phone and/or will make an appearance at residence if he is unable to reach you. If you are unable to accept delivery of your shipment within the free waiting time (i.e., two hours) after notification of the mover's arrival at the destination, you may request waiting time until delivery can be made.
- *Look For Damage or Missing Items*: Check your household goods as they are unloaded. If there is a change in the condition of the property from that noted on the inventory at the time of loading or if any items are missing, note discrepancies on the van operator's copy of the inventory sheet. By signing the inventory sheet, you are acknowledging receipt of all items listed. Personally report any loss or damage to your salesperson or move coordinator.
- *What To Expect*: When unloading, each piece of furniture will be placed as you direct, including the laying of rugs and setting up any beds disassembled at the point of origin. However, mattresses will not be unpacked, and appliances and/or fixtures will not be installed. At your request and at an additional charge, your mover can arrange for this service. The mover is not obligated to rearrange your furniture.
- *A Floor Plan Can Help The Movers*: Place a floor plan by the entrance, which the movers can use to determine where each piece of furniture should go.
- *Visit The Post Office*: Check with your new post office for any mail being held and ask for delivery to start.
- *Confirm Auto License and Registration*: Check state (and local) laws for auto registration and driver's license requirements.
- *Meet With An Attorney*: You may want to select an attorney to discuss laws that pertain to your destination state, county, and/or city. Be sure to cover such matters as wills, transfers of property and investments, insurance regulations, inheritance laws, taxes, etc. Most laws affect a family as soon as residence in the new state and city is established.
- *Store Moving Documents*: After the move is completed, keep all documents pertaining to your move in a safe place. You will need them for verification of moving expenses when you file your federal income tax returns.

NOTE: For a complete listing of *Moving Definitions and Terminology*, see Chapter 24: *Home Downsizing Resources.*

Chapter 22

Meet the Cleanout Specialist

Everyone wants the good stuff. No one wants the junk. That's where the *Cleanout Specialist* comes in. The *Cleanout Specialist* will take it all...*the good, the bad, and the junk*...for a price. *Cleanout Specialists* are sometimes called Junk Dealers, but they are often more than that. They are one of the last resources that you may need when downsizing and finally moving from your house.

What is *a Cleanout?* A cleanout can be pretty much what you want it to be. If you need a few pieces of furniture taken away, that's a cleanout. If you need a room or a garage totally cleaned out, that's a cleanout. And if you need an entire house emptied, that's also a cleanout.

Some *cleanouts* are easy and will fit into the back of a car or van. Some require a moving truck. And we have even seen one that was so large that no Cleanout Specialist wanted to handle it. There was too much junk for them to handle, and the owner wasn't willing to pay the price needed to clean the place out. So the owner sold the place "*as is*", with all of the junk in place. The new owners brought in a bulldozer and front-end loader, razed the entire building, and hauled the building and contents away in dumpsters and dump trucks.

How Do Cleanout Specialists Work? Basically they will take away whatever you don't want. They will perform the manual labor needed to cart it away, and they will make it disappear. They may sell it for a profit, or they dispose of it at the city dump. At this point you don't really care what they do with it. You just want it gone.

Cleanout Specialists have several things that you probably don't have.
- *A Young Back*. If you are in the 50+ age group and like me, you probably can't lift as much as you used to.
- *A Van or Truck*: Cleanout Specialists will have whatever vehicles are needed to get the job done.
- *Access to a Labor Pool*. Cleanouts are hard and dirty work and relatively few people want to handle them. Cleanout Specialists know where to hire whatever labor is needed to get the job done.
- *Product Knowledge*: Although they won't tell you this, Cleanout Specialists know the difference between treasures and junk. Almost every cleanout offers one or more treasures that the owner has missed, and frequently more money will be made off of this single treasure than off of the entire cleanout.
- *Disposal Capabilities*. They know where to dump the junk at the cheapest price.

161

- *Selling Capabilities*: They know where to sell all levels of items, including high end, middle market, and low end merchandise, in order to receive the maximum return for their work.

Depending upon what you have, Cleanout Specialists will typically offer you one of three options:
- *They can make you a cash offer*. If you have better merchandise, the type that offers the highest potential return for the least amount of effort, they will pay you for the merchandise.
- *They can haul it away for no money...but at no charge*. There may be some better items and some junk, and they will try to make their profit on the sellable items, while dumping the junk they don't want.
- *They can charge you to haul it away*. If it's mostly junk, they will charge you to take it away because there is little profit in the job otherwise.

Although you may not see it, Cleanout Specialists have considerable expenses when dealing with your merchandise, and those expenses must be factored into how much they will charge you.
- Labor is the greatest expense in cleanouts.
- The price of gas, vehicles, and nearly everything else is going up.
- They may incur storage costs while sorting and preparing to dispose of the merchandise.
- They will incur commissions and fees when selling the sellable items.
- They may incur dumping fees when disposing of the junk.
- Yes, they must also make a fair profit for their work.

When Are Cleanouts Appropriate? Ask yourself these five questions about a possible cleanout.
1) Have you been successful in disposing of the items elsewhere?
2) Do you want the merchandise any longer?
3) Do you know where to dispose of the merchandise?
4) Do you have a truck large enough to move it?
5) Can you get rid of the merchandise yourself?

If you answered *"No"* to each of these questions, a Cleanout may be appropriate.

Home Downsizing Tips

✓ The Cleanout Specialist will often be the final step in the *Home Downsizing* process.

✓ When dealing with the Cleanout Specialist, clearly specify that you want your job left *"Broom Cleaned"*. That means everything goes...and the cleanout person sweeps up all remaining dirt and dust. Anything less than *"Broom Cleaned"* could leave you with a bigger mess than you expected.

✓ If you communicate clearly with the Cleanout Specialist, if you spell out exactly what you want, you should have few problems in this final stage.

Chapter 23

Relax. It's Finally Over.

That's it. You're done. You've completed your *Home Downsizing in Four Easy Steps*. Take a deep breath. You've earned it.

You've completed the 4-*Step AVID Home Downsizing System*™. And in doing so you've...

- *Analyzed Your Situation*
- *Valued Your Personal Property Assets*
- *Investigated Your Selling & Disposition Options*
- *Disposed of Your Excess and Unwanted Items*

And if you've moved, you mostly likely have:

- *Packed*
- *Dealt with the Moving Company*
- *Dealt with the Cleanout Specialist*

Most likely, you've kept the best and most important items for the next phase of your life. What do you do now? Relax. Enjoy. Do what you dreamed of doing at the start of this *Home Downsizing* process. Travel. Read. Start a new career. Live a long and fruitful life.

* * * * *

If you found *Home Downsizing In Four Easy Steps* helpful, let us know.

Or better yet, tell a friend. Because although the *Home Downsizing* process can be difficult, the *AVID Home Downsizing System*™ does works...and it can make the entire *Home Downsizing* process easier for nearly everyone who uses it.

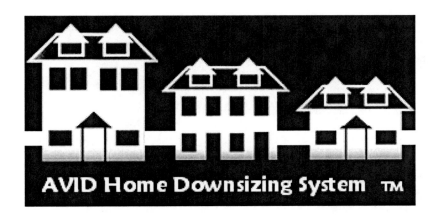

Chapter 24

Home Downsizing Resources

Tools of the Trade
- Antiques Shops
- Antiques Shows
- Auctioneers
- Auction Houses
- AVID Home Downsizing System
- Church Sales
- Cleanout Specialists
- Collector Clubs
- Consignment Shops
- Dumpster
- Favorite Charities
- Flea Markets
- Garage and Tag Sales
- Home Downsizing Consultant
- Real Estate Agents
- Thrift Shops
- Valuation Tools

Valuation Tools
- Antique Dealers
- Antiques Shops
- Antique Shows
- Appraisers
- Auctioneers
- Consignment Shops
- Fee Internet Web Sites
- Flea Markets
- Free Internet Web Sites
- Price Guides
- Search Engines
- Trade Papers
- Web Sites

Popular Free Internet Research Web Sites
- *eBay*   www.eBay.com
- *Live Auctioneers*   www.LiveAuctioneers.com
- *Sotheby's*   www.Sothebys.com
- Christie's   www.Christies.com
- *Heritage Auctions*   www.ha.com
- *Maine Antiques Digest*   www.maineantiquedigest.com
- *eBay Stores*   www.ebay.com
- *The Internet Antique Store* www.tias.com
- *Collector Online*   www.collectoronline.com

- *The Association of Collecting Clubs* www.collectors.org

Popular Fee Internet Research Sites
- *Prices for Antiques*: www.P4A.com
- *Price Miner*: www.PriceMiner.com
- *Ask Art*: www.AskArt.com
- *Art Fact*: www.ArtFact.com
- *Art Net*: www.ArtNet.com
- *Art Price*: www.ArtPrice.com
- *Gordon's Art*: www.Gordonsart.com

Disposition Options
- Dump It
- Donate It
- Keep It
- Sell It...at a Garage Sale
- Sell It...at a Tag Sale
- Sell It...at a Flea Market
- Sell It...at an Antique Shop
- Sell It...at an Antique Show
- Sell It...Privately
- Sell It...on eBay Yourself
- Sell It...through an eBay Drop Shop
- Sell It... at Auction

The Art of Negotiating

Life is full of negotiations. As a child you probably negotiated with your parents, perhaps about the size of your allowance or the amount of vegetables that you could leave on your plate. Perhaps you negotiated with a teacher on a grade. You probably negotiated with your children on what they were allowed to wear to school, or how late they could stay out at night. You probably negotiated when you purchased your car and your home. And you probably still negotiate with your spouse or partner about whether you will watch a love story or sporting event on TV.

When it comes time to privately sell your *Personal Property*, negotiation will be expected. Be prepared for it, and formulate a bargaining strategy, because if you fail to do this the buyer will almost always get the better end of the deal.

Negotiating is an art, not a science. If you understand how to negotiate, and if you understand some very basic negotiating principals and strategies, you will most likely win...because most people are unskilled at negotiating. Most don't like to negotiate, and hence fail to achieve the best selling price.

Books have been written about negotiating so I am not going to repeat what has been written elsewhere here. Rather I will give you some very basic principals that you should understand about negotiating.

- *Negotiation Is Part of the Game*: Anticipate it, prepare for it, and learn how to do it well.
- *Know What You Want*: Successful negotiators know what they want out of a deal... prior to entering into negotiations. By knowing what you are trying to accomplish, you will have a better chance of coming out on top.
- *Recognize What The Other Side Wants*: Not everyone wants the same thing out of a deal. Some are more interested in the money, other are concerned about timing, condition, prestige, or some other extraneous factors. If you understand what the other side wants, you will have a greater likelihood of coming out ahead.
- *Allow Them To Make A Profit*: It's perfectly acceptable for the buyer to make a fair profit off this transaction. But you don't want to be taken to the cleaners.
- *Win-Win Deals Are The Best*: The best deal is a *"Win-Win"* deal where both sides win, no one loses, and both walk away from the table happy.
- *Find Some Common Ground*: The key to negotiating is to final some common ground on which a deal can be made.
- *Time Matters in Negotiating*: The individual with the most time will usually win. If you wait until the last minute to sell your *Personal Property*, and if your opponent knows it, they can wait you out and you will most likely be forced to accept a lower price.
- *Knowledge Matters*: The more knowledgeable you are about what you are selling, and the state of the current market, the better deal you will be able to negotiate.
- *Have A Fall-Back Position*: You will be in a stronger negotiating position if you have a fall-back position. Three offers on the table are always better than only one.
- *Be Fair*: People prefer to work with other people who are fair. They want to stick it to jerks. If you are fair during negotiations, most likely your opponent will be fair with you.
- *Keep Focused*: Keep focused upon your goals and priorities. Is money more important to you, or where your collection is going, or how quickly it will be picked up?

Here are some helpful negotiating tactics to help you get ready.
- *Be Prepared*: Strategize, and understand the facts about what you are dealing with.
- *Never Be The First To Name A Price*. Once you reveal your anticipated price, there is only one way it can go...down.
- *Let The Buyer Name Their Price First*: Force your opponent to name the price they are willing to offer. It may be higher than the price you are expecting.
- *Don't Accept the First Offer*. Always provide a counter-offer that is 25%-50% higher than the offer you received. You will probably meet somewhere in the middle.
- *Give and Take*: Do not give anything away without asking for something in return. If they ask for a price concession, ask for an earlier payment date.
- *Let Your Opponent Save Face*. If you embarrass or ridicule your opponent, you will probably lose them as a prospective buyer.
- *Know When To Fold*. Sometimes your opponent is simply looking to steal your items at a bargain price, never intending to come close to paying fair value. It is perfectly acceptable to walk away from such a deal. But do it politely. Insulting your opponent will accomplish nothing.

Can you master these very basic but very important negotiating phrases?
- *Can you do any better?*
- *Is that your best offer?*

- *I was hoping to receive <<<50% above their offer>>>*. Can we meet somewhere in the middle?
- *If I accept your offer, will you have it out of here tomorrow?*
- *If I reduce price, will you pay for shipping?*
- *If I meet you halfway, will you pay half of the shipping?*
- *If I reduce my price, will you pay me in cash?*
- *I can accept your lower offer if you allow me to pull <<<the best 2 or 3 items>>> out of the deal.* (The buyer will usually counter-offer).

Remember that negotiating is a game. Approach it as a game, have fun with it, and you will most likely make yourself significantly more money in any deal.

HOME DOWNSIZING TIP: You can sometimes hire someone to negotiate for you. And if they can negotiate more money for you than they will charge for their services, you can come out considerably ahead.

Delivery Options
- United States Postal Service
- UPS and/or UPS Stores
- Federal Express, DHL, and other Shipping and Delivery Companies
- Buyer Pick-Up
- Deliver It Yourself

Auction Definitions and Terminology
- *Absentee Bid*: A bid that the Auctioneer executes for someone who is interested in bidding, but is unable to attend the actual Auction.
- *Absolute Auction*: An Auction without limit or reserve.
- *Appraisal*: A written or verbal opinion of value rendered by a qualified individual.
- *As Is, Where Is*: A term that means you are buying something as it currently is, and you cannot return it for any reason.
- *Auctioneer*: The individual who conducts the actual Auction. Certain states require that Auctioneers be licensed by the state and bonded.
- *Auction House*: This usually refers to either an Auction Company, or the Auction Company's place of business. An Auction House is a business entity and not an individual.
- *Auction School:* A school where prospective Auctioneers go to learn how to become an Auctioneer.
- *Bid Increments*: Normal bidding increments used by the Auctioneer, These can vary by the item, and can even vary in the sale of a single item. In the case of a "$10 bid increment", the bidding would go "$10-$20-$30, etc".
- *Box Lot*: A grouping of items, generally inexpensive ones, that are sold as a group, and often in a box, for a single bid
- *Buyer's Choice*: When an Auctioneer sells a grouping of similar items as "*Buyer's Choice*", the winning bidder can take one, some, or all of the items at the winning bid price.
- *Buyer's Premium*. Most Auctioneers charge a Buyer's Premium today, This is an amount, typically a percentage of the final selling price, that the buyer must pay to

the Auctioneer. With a 10% Buyer's Premium, a winning bidder would pay the Auctioneer $110 on a $100 winning bid.

- *By the Piece*: Occasionally Auctioneers will sell similar pieces "*by the piece*". This means that rather than selling all items for one single price, the winning bidder pays the final selling price, times the number of pieces. (e.g., 5 items at $10 per piece, $50 total).
- *Chant*: The Auctioneers chant is the rhythmic manner in which different Auctioneers sell. Auctioneers use a chant in order to sell more quickly, yet in a manner that the bidders clearly understand.
- *Commission*: The fee that an Auctioneer charges for selling a consignor's merchandise. Usually the commission is either a Flat Percentage or a Sliding Scale Commission based upon an item's final selling price.
- *Consignor*: Someone who consigns merchandise to an Auction.
- *Escrow Account*: A special bank account that some states require an Auctioneer to deposit Auction proceeds into. The purpose of an Escrow Account is to prevent an Auctioneer from comingling personal funds and consignors funds.
- *Hammer Price*: The final selling price of an item at Auction.
- *Lot*: Each time the Auctioneer says "*Sold*". A lot can be a single item, or multiple items sold for one single price.
- *On Site Auction*: An Auction held on the premises of the consignor.
- *One Money*: Occasionally Auctioneers will sell similar pieces as a group, for "*one money*" This means that the winning bidder pays one single price for the entire grouping.
- *Reserve Price*. This is the minimum selling price that an item must achieve before the consignor is required to pass title along to the winning bidder, Most items sell at Auction without a Reserve Price.
- *Sales Tax*. In most states the Auctioneer will be obliged to collect sales tax on each item they sell. Generally the only exceptions are if the item is sold to a registered dealer who is buying exclusively for re-sale, or if the item is being shipped to a winning bidder from out of state (e.g., Internet Sales).
- *Shill Bidder*: An illegal bidder in the audience who fraudulently works in conjunction with a crooked Auctioneer to inflate the final selling price on certain items.
- *Starting Bid*: This first bid received by the Auctioneer.
- *Telephone Bid*: Occasionally when someone is interested in bidding on a major item, but is unable to attend the actual Auction, the Auctioneer will make arrangements for them to bid live-time over the telephone.

Moving Definitions and Terminology

Here is a list of moving terms that you're likely to come across. If you familiarize yourself with these, you'll feel more confident in your negotiations with the mover. These definitions are taken from U.S. Department of Transportation documentation and should give you enough information to help you to select a moving company.

- *Advance Charges*: These are charges for services performed by someone other than the mover. A professional, craftsman, or other third party may perform these services at your request. The mover pays for these services and adds the charges to your Bill of Lading charges.
- *Agent*: A local moving company authorized to act on behalf of a larger, national company.

- *Bill of Lading*: The receipt for your goods and the contract for their transportation.
- *Carrier*: The moving company transporting your household goods.
- *Declared Value*: The usually self-reported value of all of the items that you are moving. It's important to be as accurate as possible because the insurance will be based on this amount.
- *Estimate, Binding*: This is an agreement made in advance with your mover. It guarantees the total cost of the move based upon the quantities and services shown on the estimate. Note: you should *always* try to get a written moving estimate, even if it is non-binding.
- *Estimate, Non-Binding*: This is what your mover believes the cost will be, based upon the estimated weight of the shipment and the accessorial services requested. A non-binding estimate is not binding on the mover. The final charges will be based upon the actual weight of your shipment, the actual services provided, and the tariff provisions in effect.
- *Expedited Service*: Expedited service is an upgraded service that guarantees delivery by a specific date. This is not standard and if you do not opt for expedited service, you should treat the "*delivery date*" as an approximate date.
- *Full Replacement Value Coverage*: Insurance coverage that fully covers the entire replacement value of your goods. This is not standard and will cost you extra (generally quoted in dollars per $1,000 of replacement value).
- *Full Service Move*: The most common kind of move, in which the moving company moves all of your items out of your current residence and into your new residence.
- *Guaranteed Pick-Up and Delivery Service*: A premium service that guarantees pick up and delivery dates (your mover will provide reimbursement to you for delays). Often subject to minimum weight requirements.
- *High Value Article*: These are items included in a shipment valued at more than $100 per pound ($220 per kilogram).
- *Line Haul Charges*: The charges for the vehicle transportation portion of your move. These charges, if separately stated, apply in addition to the accessorial service charges.
- *Long Carry*: A charge for carrying articles excessive distances between the mover's vehicle and your residence. An example might be an excessively long walk between your apartment and the elevator, Charges for these services may be in addition to the line haul charges.
- *Mobile Container*: If you do not have a full-service move you may be offered a mobile container, a large container in which you can load your stuff, usually wooden with a canvas cover. This is a less expensive way to move a small apartment, but requires more labor on your part. Great for a college move.
- *Operating Authority*: This is the official certification awarded by the government that allows a mover to move your belongings between certain areas.
- *Order (Bill of Lading) Number*: The number used to identify and track your shipment.
- *Peak Seasonal Rates*: Higher line haul charges are applicable during the summer months. This is why it is recommended you book early if you plan on moving during the summer.
- *Pick-up and Delivery Charges*: Separate transportation charges applicable for transporting your shipment between the storage-in-transit warehouse and your residence.
- *Shuttle Service*: The use of a smaller vehicle to provide service to residences not accessible to the mover's normal line haul vehicles. This usually requires double-handling and hence a higher moving rate.

- *Storage In Transit (SIT)*: The temporary warehouse storage of your shipment pending further transportation, with or without notification to you (this is different than temporary storage). If you, or someone representing you, cannot accept delivery on the agreed-upon date or within the agreed-upon time period (for example, because your home is not quite ready to occupy), your mover may place your shipment into SIT without notifying you. In those circumstances, you will be responsible for the added charges for SIT service, as well as the warehouse handling and final delivery charges. Note: Your mover also may place your shipment into SIT if your mover was able to make delivery before the agreed-upon date (or before the first day of the agreed-upon delivery period), but you did not concur with early delivery. In those circumstances, your mover must notify you immediately of the SIT, and your mover is fully responsible for redelivery charges, handling charges, and storage charges.
- *Surface Transportation Board*: An agency within the U.S. Department of Transportation that regulates household goods carrier tariffs, among other responsibilities. The Surface Transportation Board's address is 1925 K Street NW., Washington, DC 20423-0001 Tele. 202-565-1674.
- *Tarriff*: A document (in whole or in part) containing rates, rules, regulations, classifications, or other provisions. The Surface Transportation Board requires that a tariff contain three specific items. First, an accurate description of the services the mover offers to the public. Second, the specific applicable rates (or the basis for calculating the specific applicable rates) and service terms for services offered to the public. Third, the mover's tariff must be arranged in a way that allows you to determine the exact rate(s) and service terms applicable to your shipment.
- *Valuation*: The degree of worth of the shipment. The valuation charge compensates the mover for assuming a greater degree of liability than is provided for in its base transportation charges.
- *Warehouse Handling*: A charge may be applicable each time SIT service is provided. Charges for these services may be in addition to the line haul charges. This charge compensates the mover for the physical placement and removal of items within the warehouse.

About the Author

Michael Ivankovich understands *Home Downsizing*. When not selling on Auction day, most of his time has been spent visiting people's homes, evaluating their *Personal Property*, and helping them to determine how best to dispose of that *Personal Property*. Over the past 35+ years he has gained considerable experience in all aspects of this business, working at various times as an:

- Antiques Dealer
- Antiques Show Exhibitor
- Appraiser
- Author
- Columnist
- eBay Live Auction Consultant
- Flea Market Dealer
- Group Antiques Shop Exhibitor
- Public Speaker

- Antiques Shop Owner
- Antiques Show Promoter
- Auctioneer
- Cleanout Specialist
- eBay Live Auctioneer
- eBay PowerSeller
- Garage Sale Specialist
- Personnel Trainer
- Tag Sale Specialist

Here are some additional facts about Mike that you may want to know:
- Author, *Home Downsizing in Four Easy Steps.*
- *Graduate Personal Property Appraiser* (1 of only 236 *GPPA's* in the U.S.).
- *Master Personal Property Appraiser* (1 of only 60 *MPPA's* in the U.S.).
- *USPAP* Certified Appraiser.
- Licensed and Bonded Auctioneer.
- Pennsylvania's *2004 Auctioneer of the Year*
- Past President, *Lehigh Valley Society of Auctioneers.*
- Author 15+ Antiques & Collectibles Books.
- Contributing Advisor to *Warman's, Schroeder's, Kovel's, Antique Trader,* and most other national Price Guides.
- Columnist whose articles have appeared in trade papers nationwide.
- Professional Antiques Dealer 35+ years.
- Past President, *Bucks County Antiques Dealers Association.*

And Mike can help you through your *Home Downsizing* process as well. He is available to help you with:
- In-Home Personal Property Walk-Through Valuations
- USPAP Appraisals
- Home Downsizing Consultations
- Packing and Cleanout Services
- Negotiations
- And pretty much anything else you may need in the Home Downsizing process.

You can contact his offices for further details at (215)-345-6094, or visit his Web Site:
www.HomeDownsizingConsultants.com

CASHING-IN ON HOME DOWNSIZING

Schedule a SEMINAR or WORKSHOP For Your Group or Organization

Michael Ivankovich, the author of this book, can conduct either a 1-hour or ½-day *Cashing-In On Home Downsizing* presentation for your group or organization. Obviously a ½-day workshop will go into significantly more detail than a 1-hour seminar, but either session will introduce your group to the *Home Downsizing* process while providing such topics as:

- *An Introduction*... To the *Home Downsizing* process.
- *20 Questions*... To ask yourself when considering a *Home Downsizing*.
- *What's It Worth?*...How to learn the value of your personal property in today's market.
- *Hidden Treasures*...How to determine if you have any in your home.
- *10 Selling & Disposition Options*...Which are available to you.
- *How and Where to Sell*...Your excess personal property for top dollar.
- *Tips & Strategies*...To make your Home Downsizing easier while at the same time saving you money.

These sessions will also introduce you to the 4-step *AVID Home Downsizing System*™ which will show you how:

- **A**nalyze...your individual Home Downsizing Situation
- **V**alue...your Personal Property Assets
- **I**nvestigate...your selling and disposition options
- **D**ispose...of all excess and unwanted items.

But most importantly, these sessions will show you how you can downsize your home...
- For the greatest amount of cash...
- With the least amount of work...
- In the shortest amount of time.

Each Workshop includes:
- *Home Downsizing Handouts & Spreadsheets*
- *Home Downsizing Tips Sheets*... with 100+ *Home Downsizing Tips & Strategies*
- Your personal *Home Downsizing Checklist*. And much more.

If you are planning a *Home Downsizing* or move in the near future, you need to schedule a *Home Downsizing Seminar* or *Workshop* for your group or organization today.

For further details contact:
Michael Ivankovich, Home Downsizing Consultant
P.O. Box 1536 ● Doylestown, PA 18901 ● (215)-345-6094
info@HomeDownsizingConsultants.com ● www.HomeDownsizingConsultants.com